"I wanted to tell the story of all the country-ass people I grew up with. These folks are just trying to carve out a life with what they know and what they have."

Reverend Peyton, p. 54

Contents

ON THE COVER

The American heartland is so named because it occupies the center of the country geographically. It's also where much of our food is grown and where many of our domestically made goods are manufactured. Musically, it's where countless consequential American artists have made their way — Bob Dylan, John Mellencamp, Melissa Etheridge, Bright Eyes, the Jayhawks, and Robbie Fulks among them. So we thought it was time to turn our focus away from Nashville, New York, and Austin, toward the heart of the country. To grace the cover, Iowan Greta Songe gave us this beautiful landscape, where a fiddler plays while a tractor rolls, and back in those hills, something's brewing.

Inside covers: Lyrics from John Mellencamp's "Little Pink Houses," by Drew Christie

Dear Reader,

You hold in your hands the latest copy of *No Depression* — a quarterly journal published by the FreshGrass Foundation. The FreshGrass Foundation is a 501(c)3 nonprofit organization dedicated to preserving and promoting the past, present, and future of American roots music through this journal, nodepression.com, the FreshGrass Festival, and an assortment of giving programs. Among our giving programs is the No Depression Writing Fellowship, which annually awards one writer a $10,000 fellowship to spend a full year digging into a single story. At the back of this issue, you'll find the first installment from our 2017 writing fellow, Sarah Smarsh, who will spend this year writing 40,000 words about Dolly Parton's influence on working-class feminism. To learn more about this and other FreshGrass Foundation giving programs — including how you can support the foundation — visit freshgrass.org. If you've subscribed to this journal, your dollars are already helping to fund the foundation's work, and we will be telling you more in the coming months about how you can do more, and what we plan to do with these funds. For now, I just wanted to take a moment to thank you for supporting roots music.

Sincerely,
Chris Wadsworth
Publisher of *No Depression* and Founder of the FreshGrass Foundation

NO DEPRESSION TEAM
Chris Wadsworth *Publisher*
Kim Ruehl *Editor-in-Chief*
Stacy Chandler *Assistant Editor*
Cameron Matthews *Editor of NoDepression.com*
Sonja Nelson *Advertising*
Henry Carrigan *Print Partnerships*
Maureen Cross *Finance/Operations*

WEB nodepression.com
TWITTER & INSTAGRAM @nodepression
FACEBOOK facebook.com/nodepressionmag

GENERAL INQUIRIES
info@nodepression.com

ONLINE ADVERTISING
advertising@nodepression.com

SUBSCRIPTIONS
nodepression.com/subscribe

JOURNAL DESIGN & PRODUCTION
Marcus Amaker
Printed in Canada by Hemlock Printers , 100% carbon neutral

No Depression is part of the FreshGrass Foundation.
freshgrass.org
ISBN: 978-0-9973317-5-2
©2017, FreshGrass, LLC

Hello Stranger

BY KIM RUEHL

About a week after last November's presidential election, I started getting emails from writers who were working on stories for this issue, asking for extensions. Though a couple of them had to do  with the typical things — tracking down sources, verifying facts — most were more along the lines of, "I just need a couple extra days to wrap my head around this new reality."

Of course, with a little space from the initial shock, it's easy to recognize that there is no such thing as a "new" reality. We live in the same country today that we occupied on November 7, 2016, though those of us on the coasts would certainly do well to reckon with our sense of privilege and power, and our ideas about America in general.

After the last president was elected, we heard talk about the influence of the urban archipelago, a configuration of coastal cities that held much of the nation's population and hence the most political sway. Of course, the ensuing eight years didn't exactly bear that out, as representatives from places like Kansas, Wisconsin, and Kentucky categorically blocked the policies attempted by a progressive president who had graduated from Ivy League schools on the East Coast and was elected by folks in that urban archipelago.

So the pendulum swings, and here we are. (The reassuring thing about a pendulum is that it is always tethered to something.)

America is huge. In a former life, I drove all over it, singing songs, exploring. Boston to Orlando, Western New York to Northwest Oregon, Brooklyn to New Orleans, Portland to Los Angeles, Flagstaff to Seattle. I road Greyhound buses from Central Florida to Washington State, up and down the East Coast more times than I can count. I've driven I-10 through Texas and I've circled the central states from Denver to Utah, Utah to Montana, West Virginia to Wisconsin.

These are not just the names of places. They are communities of people who are bound together (or if you choose, separated) by Eisenhower's highways. The people who live in these places gather at the gas station, the hardware store, the Waffle House or Denny's parking lot, the Wal-Mart, the record store, the airfield, the barn, the tavern. Growing up they shoot squirrels and beer cans, get stoned and play Dylan tunes, go camping, sit on the corner and get real bored, watch the world go by, talk shit, fall in love, fall out of love, get afraid, overcome, feel like they're flying. Just like I did growing up, way out on the East Coast.

In the weeks and months since the election, I've read the thinkpieces and the tweets and all the other stuff. I've seen stories wielded like surgical tools, bisecting our belief systems and ideas, our emotions and our landscapes into various "us"-es and "them"s. There are the liberals and the conservatives, the religious and the secular, the wealthy and the poor, the studious and the undereducated — and of course the coastal elites and the Midwesterners. But in all my travels, I've never met the people those stories talk about. I've met people who love Hank and Merle and Dolly, Steve and Bruce and Woody. People who like to look at fireworks and love it when the guitar is cranked up loud. People who see magic in fireflies and the way the sky churns ahead of a summer storm. People who want their kids to have it a little bit easier than they did.

So while I'll concede that stories about division can be pretty powerful, I also know they're not true. There's a reason that one word for a good long story is a "yarn." That the elements that connect a narrative are called "threads." Ultimately stories are here for us to be drawn closer to one another, to experience the ways in which our lives are interwoven, knitted together.

We hadn't intended to start the year with an issue exploring what the coastal media has come to call "Trump's America." But the stories unveiled their own threads. Here are the neighborhoods of Ohio, Indiana, Wisconsin, Michigan, Minnesota, Iowa, Kansas, Missouri, and Montana about which so much has been written lately. Here are the stories beyond the smoke and mirrors, about the social fabric of those communities, the threads that tie them together, and the ways that music — this same music that moves us all — brings light into every room it enters.

NO DEPRESSION

A View from the Second City

by Robbie Fulks

MOVED FROM NEW YORK TO Chicago at 20. I had rarely left the East Coast, and my impressions of the Midwest came from novels and stereotypes. A lot of the funny people I admired — Garrison Keillor, Bill Murray, David Letterman — came from that region, as did much of the masthead of my beloved *National Lampoon*; but what all these sensibilities shared was hard to pinpoint. Aloofness? My boss at the midtown Manhattan publishing firm where I worked, an explosively ill-tempered runt named Don Fine, spoke simple words when he learned where I was headed. "Chicago's a hick town!" he asserted. "You won't have any trouble there."

About the trouble he was right. Apartments in Chicago in 1983 were cheap, parking plentiful and often free. The winters were long and ugly but also had an aspect of majesty. With stoic solidarity, Chicagoans bore up under some of the ruder ordnance in nature's arsenal. The geography of the North Shore — Green Bay Road snaking parallel to the tracks of the commuter line, itself mirroring the coastline of Lake Michigan — was softly dazzling, as a raft of snowglobey scenes in John Hughes movies was soon to memorialize. Downtown, the "L" wheezed circularly like a dilapidated Coney Island ride. Newspaper men like Mike Royko and Bob Greene sat in pupil-enlarging, cigar-choked bars at midday. Gimlet-eyed workers stomped through sooty slush. Each morning I bought a *Tribune* and sat in a toilet stall of the Greyhound station marking want ads. I found an okay-paying job doing boring work at a law firm within a few weeks.

Nights, I played at clubs in then-bohemian Lincoln Park, places like Holstein's and Orphans. They weren't hard to get booked in. A year after my move, I began teaching at the Old Town School of Folk Music, and a year after that quit my day job to play guitar for Special Consensus, then as now the only bluegrass act in town with a national profile, which it toured nonstop to maintain. At that point I became what I've been ever since and will probably die being: a Chicago-based working musician. Try moving to New York with no particular brains or skills, getting a nice apartment, and becoming a working musician in three years. (Actually, I had tried that.)

Second-rate Syndrome

If you're based in a mid-Atlantic state, you can route major cities almost at random — Richmond, Baltimore, Philadelphia, Boston — and your drive times will stay reasonable. With a little stamina, you can even avoid a hotel stay. Though the distances are brief, the Eastern cities are at a marked cultural remove from one another. By contrast, in the Midwest you drive 4 to 8 hours to arrive at places that have at least a cousin-strength resemblance in topography, weather, and manners to your departure point. Cleveland, Columbus, Indianapolis, Louisville, Knoxville, St. Louis, Milwaukee, Madison, Iowa City, the two Bloomingtons, Ann Arbor, Omaha: the towns are like soft-bordered squares in a homely, harmonious quilt.

A Chicago base brings a challenge, however. As a theater director in Sue Miller's novel *The Lake Shore Limited* says: "What happens in Chicago stays in Chicago." "Famous people just don't live in Chicago," an L.A. personality complained to me once (a little insultingly, since he had asked me to appear as a guest on his podcast during its Chicago visit). Actors here have seen casting agents separate out from a stack of resumes the serious candidates, those with New York addresses in the top corner. A music promoter once advised me in organizing a program for a venue: "No Chicago musicians, for God's sake!"

Saul Bellow defined Chicago as the city where they love you after you've made it in New York. That's close to how it worked out for me: I drew so-so in small clubs for my first 13 years in Chicago; only after I had gone to the majors and gained an audience elsewhere was I set. If there's a superstition that second-city art is second-rate, the headquarters for the heresy is right here, unfortunately. The first thing we Chicagoans can do to improve our cultural position is to stop celebrating ourselves so ardently, insecurely, and constantly. Chicago's the only place where a show will kick off with an emotional speech from a venue manager, radio personality, or politician about how great Chicago is. Yikes. Shut up and show something.

Glue People Together

I lodged the Morells (they later rebooted as the Skeletons) in my mind after hearing or reading that they were a "heartland NRBQ," a rather dull medal they were awarded by dull writers. Like Christ our Savior, the great winter of 1979, and Professor Irwin Corey, NRBQ was a category with only itself as a member. One of my first inklings of the Midwest's otherness was in 1984, when the 'Q, a cherished fixture back east, were booked at Cabaret Metro and then canceled after only 18 tickets were presold. Later that year I bought the Morells' *Shake and Push* LP. Led by a lean, bald-headed, pot-smoking populist named Lou Whitney, the Springfield, Missouri, band joined two opposed aesthetics, old-pro skill and teenage zest, and they essayed multiple styles. All like NRBQ — but where their easterly brethren embraced avant-gardism and theatricality, offering themselves as rock stars, the Morells were defiantly ordinary. You knew they were pro-union Democrats because they had a song that said so. They were fondly attached to their town, a small eccentric place; they wrote about it and covered local songwriters like Ronnie Self and Wayne Carson. Comfortable in their skins, Lou and his bandmates (one of them was his wife, a nutty middle-aged lady in short pants) projected minimal performative self-awareness on stage. They wore what they might wear to go buy medicine at Walgreens.

Lou's dead now, and the band dispersed a lot of years ago. For me the magic midpoint of the line segment whose ends are "first falling in love with the Morells" and that previous sentence is the year 1995, when I started working with them and we all became friends. Lou

was someone around whom anyone could relax. He had a princely authority emanating from his body language — tall frame, loose shoulders, bouncing gait — and a steady hail of witty persiflage. He loved his neighborhood, and was always loaning out gear and time at his South Street studio to struggling businesses or young whippersnappers of no discernible talent who wanted to learn the ropes or just receive the thrill of hearing themselves on tape. ("I like to drop acid once a year," he remarked, "to keep in touch with the kids.")

He was a little professorial, and he liked taking charge. At a mom-and-pop Italian place, he'd grab your condiments, small bowls of garlic and grated Parmesan, and mix them together, even if you hadn't said, "I don't know how to mix two kinds of food together; would you please show me?" If you told him, as I did, that your politics ran libertarian, he'd shoot back, "Wanna know why that'll never work?" and explain how the GI Bill saved America. If you told him, as I again did, that you were going to release music on your own, without an outside label's help, he'd say, "You wanna know why putting out records from your dining room table will never work?" It was sometimes a bit much, but his good humor always won out. He used his imposing personality to glue people together, not push them around.

What It Looks Like

If there's anything different about Midwesterners, maybe it's because the land around us looks as it does. Economic forces, which help give cities their look, are implied. My friend Scott, who plays in the current version of NRBQ, says the big difference between the coasts and us is that we don't have charming small towns. It's true: our small towns are by and large

depressing and hollowed-out. Work takes me through places like Mansfield, Ohio; Benton Harbor, Michigan; Mt. Vernon, Illinois. Not charming. I think about what I see in these places and write songs about it. It's stark and lonely and hard to get out of your mind.

Hardluck towns — of which one of the most pleasant things you can say is

Try moving to New York with no particular brains or skills, getting a nice apartment, and becoming a working musician in three years. (Actually, I had tried that.)

there's no entertainment business in them — draw out definite traits in people. Bitterness, naturally. Boastfulness. Resentment against people in loftier places who talk down to us — and as payback from us, please enjoy your new president. (The election demonstrates again that Midwesterners suspect Midwesterners of being second-rate.) A reinforced chauvinism — it's ugly but I love it all the more, goddammit. A determination, if you're an extraordinary person, to be extraordinarily gracious, to rise and lift others with you.

A melancholy memory I have is from a documentary about Lou that the journalist Dave Hoekstra started making a while back. In it, Lou, sick with cancer, stands on a sunny street, recalling when Maybelle Carter and the Carter Sisters lived in town, temporarily, during the long-ago reign of the *Ozark Jubilee* TV variety show. "I think it's pretty cool that the Carters — the Carters! — lived here, right in Springfield," he says, gesturing behind him. But he's pointing at a vacant lot. ∎

ANDY GOODWIN

FROM THE GROUND UP

Chicago Farmer has built his career close to home

by Jonathan Bernstein

FOR FOLKSINGER CODY Diekhoff, who has been performing under the name Chicago Farmer since 2002, singing songs about the people and places in his home state of Illinois is simply part of the job description. "That's what folk music is," he says. "It's music about the people who exist in the world around you."

Ever since he released his debut album, *About Time*, in 2005, he has been working off the thesis that folk music is a fundamentally local art form that, at its best, converses and engages with its surroundings. In the decade since, he has filled his ever-growing body of work with tongue-in-cheek, locally focused tunes like "Illinois Anthem" and "26 Cops" from 2006. There was "Mackinaw Girl" in 2011, his paean to local love, and 2013's small-town ode "Everybody in This Town." Across his seven albums to date, Diekhoff has quietly but steadily amassed one of the most formidable local singer-songwriter catalogs in the greater Midwest.

"Cody's about as central Illinois as you get — when he sings about it, people relate," says Edward David Anderson, lead singer of Backyard Tire Fire and another artist who has become a pillar of the fast-growing central Illinois roots music community over the last decade.

Diekhoff was born and raised in the tiny farming town of Delavan, Illinois. He moved to Chicago as a young adult and later settled closer to Delavan, in Bloomington, where he lives today. "[Central Illinois] is really his place," Anderson says. "This is where he cut his teeth. It's where he learned how to ride a bike, where he learned how to play a guitar, where he had his first kiss, and that comes out clearly in his songs. He sings about what he knows, and he does it really well."

Where It's Coming From

Chicago Farmer's music primarily draws from a mix of folk, bluegrass, and country. Diekhoff is a versatile singer whose vocals can recall both the relaxed warmth of Mason Jennings and the high nasal twang of Robbie Fulks. But onstage, he most closely resembles Todd Snider, effortlessly weaving stories and drawn-out artistic mission statements into his stage act with enthusiasm and drama. His manager, Chad Staehly, a member of Great American Taxi who now plays in Snider's band Hard Working Americans, introduced the two a few years back.

After opening for Snider a handful of times, Diekhoff now considers him an informal mentor of sorts. "When somebody like Todd tells you that you've got something and should keep pursuing it, that makes you want to pull out your guitar and keep going," he says.

In 2017, Diekhoff finds himself at a transitional moment. Chicago Farmer's new album, *Midwest Side Stories*, released last fall, is his most ambitious, far-reaching album to date. It's full of the type of adventurous arrangements and mature song craftsmanship that is bound to complete his decade-long transformation from central Illinois favorite to regional Midwestern stalwart to nationally renowned singer-songwriter. Although it contains a great deal of central Illinois-specific themes and narratives — including a devastating account of the local heroin epidemic ("Rocco N' Susie") and a loving dedication to the region's labor history ("Farms & Factories") — there is also a clear attempt at incorporating broader national concerns on *Midwest Side Stories*.

For example, "Two Sides of the Story," a politically charged critique of partisan polarization that serves as the centerpiece of the album, begins by alluding to the shooting of Michael Brown by a police officer in Ferguson, Missouri:

*A young man out walking
In the city summer heat
In the middle of America
In the middle of the street.*

"This new album connects more with the times we live in right now, nationwide," says Diekhoff. "People can relate to it on a wide scale."

He adds that the larger social problems he sees in his community — working class economic anxiety, racially motivated police shootings, paralyzing opiate addiction, increased political polarization — are problems that are affecting the entire country.

"When the Ferguson thing happened," he says, "it made me realize how divided our country really is. These things happen so close by to everyone, whether you're in Chicago or Ferguson or Cleveland or Minneapolis. Even if you're from a small town, like I am, these big cities are so close by, so you can relate."

He has a line he likes to say to the audience when he's introducing himself during his set. It's a simple enough declaration, but it serves as an apt statement of purpose for the singer: "I write songs about small towns, big cities, and everywhere in between."

As he takes aim at broadening his appeal, Diekhoff is not at all concerned about losing his connection with the central Illinois community in the transition. "Even if I try to expand or experiment with new things, people around here will still get it," he says. "They'll know that it's coming from the heart, and even though I'm trying new things and going out on a limb, they'll still know where it's coming from."

Plainspoken Music

Diekhoff began writing songs on a whim. He was sitting in study hall in high school one day when, for no particular reason at all, he started scribbling down lyrics. "I fell in love with the words, they just came out. I didn't have to search for them," says Diekhoff, who still considers himself a lyrics-first songwriter. "My whole thing is putting the poetry into

motion. I love the music ... but lyrics are kind of my thing."

He came of age during the '90s, was heavy into grunge and hardcore as a teenager: Fugazi, Metallica, Minor Threat. At home, his parents listened to classic rock like Led Zeppelin and the Beatles and blues-rock like Ten Years After. But as he spent his teenage afternoons listening to hard rock in his friend's upstairs bedroom, he found himself slowly beginning to fall for the faint, high-lonesome melodies that came drifting upward from the Hank Williams covers his friend's father would play downstairs on an acoustic guitar. Eventually, Diekhoff started going downstairs to hear his friend's father play this strangely plain-spoken music that was unlike anything he had ever heard before. "I started to get more out of the guy with just a guitar than I was from these five-piece heavy metal or punk bands coming out of the stereo upstairs," he says.

Diekhoff's love for folk and roots music only intensified when he moved to Chicago in his 20s. He began taking harmonica lessons at the city's legendary Old Town School of Folk Music, where he learned more about the city's rich folk history, primarily the early '70s, when singers like John Prine and Steve Goodman could be found gigging around town on any given night. He fell particularly hard for Prine, a fellow Chicagoan with rural family roots.

"Once I started listening to John Prine, it was all over from there," he says. His goals were set: Diekhoff would call himself Chicago Farmer, and like Prine, he was going to dedicate his life to writing and singing songs about the family members, neighbors, and friends he'd grown up with.

On Chicago Farmer's new album, traces of Diekhoff's grunge-rock roots can be heard for the first time — especially on songs like "Revolving Door" and the closing track, a cover of John

Hartford's "I'm Still Here." "Some people go back to their roots and play roots music," he says, describing the common trend of punk/rock frontmen eventually turning to folk music later in life. "I kind of did it backward and went back to my grungier, high school roots instead."

Building a Scene

Bloomington, Illinois, is a midsized Midwestern city (population 79,000) located in the dead center of the state. When Diekhoff first moved there, in 2008, there wasn't much of an established music scene. The main problem? There weren't any proper music venues in the entire city. So to play gigs during his first few years there, he and his friends created their own venues, putting together shows in garages, basements, living rooms, and coffee houses around town and promoting them by walking around downtown and hanging up homemade posters wherever they could find space on local bulletins.

"The do-it-yourself approach we had really made our musical community stronger," he says. Soon, local investors and developers recognized a growing demand for proper music venues: It was the height of the economic recession, and real estate prices were relatively affordable. Within just a couple years, clubs, bars, and auditoriums began sprouting up in both Bloomington and nearby cities like Peoria and Springfield. One such venue was the Castle Theatre, an 800-capacity venue that opened up in downtown Bloomington in the fall of 2010.

Rory O'Connor, a co-owner of the Castle Theatre who also handles booking, still remembers one moment from the venue's second-ever show, a double bill with Chicago Farmer and Backyard Tire Fire. "One of the most memorable moments I can identify was when Cody came onstage with Backyard

> **"I think the scene [in central Illinois] is thriving. My friends and I have just lost interest in big arena shows. We're into local shows because they're more affordable, and it's more of an experience."**
>
> Cody Diekhoff (Chicago Farmer)

Tire Fire to cover Neil Young's 'Rockin in the Free World' during the encore," says O'Connor. "The place got so loud that it was just this moment where I had to realize that yes, we're in this rock club business, and it's pretty awesome."

Having a midsized venue in town that consistently brought in national touring acts became a huge boon for Chicago Farmer, who landed gigs as the set opener for a wide range of touring acts all around the state. One week in 2011, he opened up for Gene Ween (lead singer of alt-rock band Ween) in Rock Island, Illinois, then three days later was back home in Bloomington opening up for bluegrasser Del McCoury.

Today, everyone seems to agree that the music scene in Bloomington has never been better. "I think the scene is thriving," says Diekhoff. "My friends and I have just lost interest in big arena shows. We're into local shows because they're more affordable, and it's more of an experience."

"The central Illinois music scene has really gotten more vibrant than it used to be," says O'Connor, who admits that competition among local venues is as tough as it's ever been, with so many having sprouted up in the last five years. "At the same time, I think it's helping some of these young bands blossom, so it's exciting to see what's going on here."

"I don't think people think of central Illinois as being this blossoming hotbed of music," adds Anderson. "But it really is."

Firmly Planted

Over the past few years, Chicago Farmer has focused on becoming a major regional act in the Midwest, developing significant fan bases in nearby cities like St. Louis and Indianapolis. One of his biggest followings is in Cincinnati, which Diekhoff says was a direct result of a local promoter finding his music on YouTube and booking him on a whim for the Whispering Beard Folk Festival in nearby Friendship, Indiana. Chicago Farmer has now played the festival six years in a row, and his relationship with it has turned Cincinnati into one of his best markets.

"As someone who considers himself a local act, the internet has been huge for me," says Diekhoff. "I really feel like I should thank Mark Zuckerberg in my liner notes, and I can't believe most musicians don't."

But for all of the tech world's evangelizing about the internet's ability to let one discover music from anywhere in the world, Chicago Farmer's career is a reminder that at its best, social media can be used as a fundamentally local tool. He has built his strong regional following thusly: internet discovery, word of mouth, fandom through local association, and, most importantly, relentless touring.

Chicago Farmer has toured major Midwest markets every year since 2010, and although he regularly plays as far west as Colorado, he has never once set foot on stages along the East Coast. It's an atypical strategy that has seemed to work: rather than play sparsely attended singer-songwriter rooms in cities like New York and Boston, at a stage where he hasn't yet developed a national following, he's been focusing his career energies on growing and strengthening his bond with the audiences who have been with him since the beginning.

As Chicago Farmer seems poised for a big 2017, his friend Edward David Anderson is excited as ever to have witnessed his friend's progress over the years.

"Cody's the guy who has continuously worked really, really hard to get where he is. Not only have I watched him grow from a musical standpoint, but from a business standpoint too. He's taken steps to put himself in a position to get some more attention nationally, and that's due to fucking fortitude," says Anderson. "All of us get told 'no' at this level a lot more than we get told 'yes,' so you just have to keep going and believe in what you're doing, and that's what he's done."

From Diekhoff's perspective, it's all about keeping it close to home. "My hometown crowds just get it," he says. "And I get them — and we get it together." ∎

MADE IN MILWAUKEE

Peter Mulvey's music is rooted in his hometown's struggles

by Erin Lyndal Martin

WHEN PETER MULVEY thinks about home, he thinks of his family, Lake Michigan, the Milwaukee neighborhood where he lives, and all that he has seen from his bike.

"Where I live absolutely informs everything about me," the singer-songwriter says. "I've lived just about the entirety of my life [here]. I don't actually play [in] Milwaukee that much, but I'm around 200 days a year. I ride my bike all over town." Every year, Mulvey bikes his way through a tour with dates primarily in Wisconsin, allowing him to see how his hometown fits in with the rest of the state.

One thing Mulvey has seen from his bike is the way economic change has affected his hometown. "Across my lifetime," he explains, "the manufacturing jobs in Milwaukee went away. Milwaukee is a lot like all the other Upper Midwest [cities]: Sort of post-industrial, very enclave-y, very neighborhood-y, ethnically divided. [There's] the Irish neighborhood, the Polish neighborhood. Even today, some of the ATMs will be in English and Spanish and Polish. When the industrial base fled, it was really rough on Milwaukee and Cleveland and Dayton and Chicago, and all those towns."

He also recalls the harsh lines that were drawn between black communities and white people, and that are still being drawn. (As recently as 2011, the Milwaukee area was considered the most segregated metropolitan area in America.) "I'm informed by the playgrounds I grew up in," he says. "I grew up on a playground where I was one of the only white kids. So I'm in the fairly rare position of being a white Wisconsinite who actually grew up around black people. If you look at the work I've done over the past couple of years, just the work that I've put out, quite a lot of it has been informed by that, and [it] has allowed me to think in a way that is tough to see if you didn't grow up in Milwaukee."

Always Music

Mulvey was raised in Sherman Park, a neighborhood in northwest Milwaukee. Originally home to some of the city's first

business owners and to many Orthodox Jews, the neighborhood now is predominantly black and South Asian. Neighborhood groups have worked since the 1970s to preserve diversity and commercial viability. It was there that Mulvey's parents, who had met as volunteers with PAVLA (Papal Volunteers for Latin America) in Belize, raised their family. His father was a social worker for the county Department on Aging, and his mother worked as an editor.

While Mulvey was influenced by his parents' service and the diversity of his community, there was never any other option for him than music. In fact, he decided around the age of ten that he was going to be a professional musician. The traditional Midwestern work ethic has fueled his ambitious songwriting, recording, and touring ever since. While he's taken short-term jobs in restaurants and factories, he has never turned away from music. Most of that music has been

on his own as well, and his albums were mostly recorded on meager budgets. He had a college band named Big Sky, and has more recently teamed up with Kris Delhmorst and Jeffrey Foucault in a trio called Redbird. He also currently has a side project, Crumbling Beauties, that performs occasionally in Massachusetts (generally performing Tom Waits' *Rain Dogs* in its entirety).

Mulvey knew he wanted to be a musician ever since he attended summer

fit onto any record. He maintains a weekly songwriting practice and cites traditional Irish music and stalwarts of American poetry among his biggest influences and inspirations.

"Mary Oliver [and] Kay Ryan [are] huge with me," he says. "Ted Kooser is great. Jim Harrison, by the way, is a wonderful poet, but he's mostly known for his novellas. ... I'm a perpetual student — being a student is huge with me. I've obsessed over 'What's Goin' On' by Marvin Gaye and the work of James Jamerson and Benny Benjamin and the themes in that record. I don't play a lot of R&B. I'm pretty voracious. A lot of my stuff is informed by things that aren't even necessarily music. I'm an avid reader of poetry, and I have volumes and volumes of poetry on my shelves. I don't expect that to change. That's the entire mission, is to just keep absorbing art. It's sort of like 'you are what you eat.'"

Through absorbing art, doing so much travel while touring, and watching different social tensions unfold in Milwaukee, Mulvey has cultivated an activist's conscience. Fortunately, that dovetails nicely with his gifts as a songwriter.

In 2015, he wanted to take action after the mass shooting at the Emanuel African Methodist Episcopal Church in Charleston, South Carolina. He wrote a song called "Take Down Your Flag," which he immediately posted online. It tells the story of Susie Jackson, who at 87 was the oldest victim of the shootings. In a creative move of collaborative activism, he invited other songwriters to write new versions for the other victims, as well verses for activists and legislators, and even one for shooter Dylann Roof.

In essence, Mulvey was turning toward social media to create a new avenue for the oral tradition of folk music. "I've been prone to just make a song and make a little video up and send it out there on the waters of social media. That's been really beautiful. It's sort of an egalitarian version of radio. I've had a few songs go out there

and be seen a hundred thousand times, apparently only on their merits. People just find it interesting and share it. ...

"Two hundred people rewrote ['Take Down Your Flag'], and over the course of several weeks it became a little movement, if I can use such a term. ... After the shootings down in Orlando, I wrote this tune called 'Jesus Wants to Take Your Guns Away' and again, same thing. It got out there and [was] shared a couple hundred thousand times."

Making Space

All of Mulvey's interests come together in his music, whether showcased in his poignant lyricism or in his versatility on the guitar. "I always really love [Peter's] lead guitar playing, although he doesn't air it out all that often," says singer-songwriter and Redbird collaborator Delmhorst. "There's a little Ireland in there, a little Tin Pan Alley, a little jazz, a little rock and roll."

For Mulvey, the key element for a good-sounding guitar is space. "Most of what I do is to try to introduce space into things, and play just a few notes to imply movement and to imply chords," he said in an interview with the Boston Beats music website. I asked him to elaborate on this, and he pointed to his role models: "I had only a little bit of schooling, but I had some good teachers. I've been a student ever since. I've just been drawn to artists that create a lot of space. I think my favorite guitar player on this earth is Bill Frisell. He has, obviously, a lot of technique. He has, obviously, a lot of vocabulary. But what I find impressive about him is the intention and the spaciousness that he brings."

Mulvey's respect for other musicians runs deep, and that shows in the trust he puts in them during recording. That trust is especially important since Mulvey lacks the budget or inclination for a lot of overdubbing. "Most of my albums have been pretty easy to make because I've been working on a shoestring for 30

camp as a child and saw a counselor there play guitar. "I got a guitar for Christmas when I was seven years old, and the very first thing I did with it was make up some story about cowboys and Indians, as a seven-year-old does. I did a lot of strumming and holding chords, which, frankly, has not changed very much, has it?"

By his own admission, Mulvey is a perpetual student, and he absorbs far more musical knowledge than could ever years," he says. "I just made a record at Ani DiFranco's house down in New Orleans. It certainly was facilitated and made easier by how tremendous of a producer she was, but the process is always the same. I go into a room with other musicians, and in a couple, three days, we tend to sit down and play these songs. I'm just not a control freak when it comes to art. If I've hired you, it's because I like how you sound. And I like the decisions you're going to make. I very rarely have any motivation to tell somebody to do something different. Just play like you play. That's why we're in a room together, because I want you to play like yourself. So it tends to go pretty quick and most of what winds up on a record is take two or take three. Sometimes even take one."

Ultimately, as we all know, good music is about far more than the sum of spacious guitars, books of poetry, and skilled production. Mulvey brings those things as well as the vital tissue of human connection to his songs, whether on his albums or in his live shows. And one wonders if the career Mulvey has made for himself as a hard-working, social justice-minded, poetry-reading troubadour would have been possible if his roots were anywhere other than Milwaukee.

In addition to the city's racial hypersegregation, its amenities are uneven, offering a confusing portrait of the town. Milwaukee consistently ranks high on lists of cities with the most poverty, yet it boasts many museums, arts centers, concert halls, universities, and other cultural amenities. It's laid out in such a way that it's easy to go quickly from the scenic Riverwalk to an impoverished and dangerous neighborhood.

Historically, Milwaukee has also been known for corruption within the police force, and those tensions have been rising again recently. A 2011 report found that at least 93 Milwaukee police officers had been disciplined for breaking the law in offenses that include sexual assault, shoplifting, domestic violence, and drunk driving. Last August, Officer Dominique

Heaggan-Brown shot and killed Sylville Smith, an armed black man, and the event sparked violent protests in the Sherman Park neighborhood. Heaggan-Brown was fired in October after being charged with sexual assault on an intoxicated man the day after the shooting.

Mulvey bears witness to all of this, hears all too much about the violence in the neighborhood where he grew up. He sees the sparkling water of Lake Michigan among civil unrest and a trenchant racial divide. The opulence of concerts at the Pabst Theater and the patchwork areas of deep poverty throughout the city. And, while touring takes Mulvey all over the globe, he feels that it deepens his understanding of home.

"I've been in the position of having traveled, of having been to Paris and London and Bethel and Anchorage, Alaska, and Duluth, Minnesota, and Lafayette, Louisiana. In a weird sense, I can say I know more about being a Wisconsinite than most people do because I have something to compare it to."

As a songwriter, he places images of his very conflicted hometown alongside the new cities he sees and the new people he meets. One of his best-known songs, "Vlad the Astrophysicist" — which may or may not be based on real events — describes a profound, existential conversation with an airplane seatmate.

Mulvey's album *Ten Thousand Mornings* was recorded in the Davis Square station of the Boston area's subway system, harkening back to a stint busking around Somerville, Massachusetts. Add to that a constant influx of poetry he reads in his email and in books, and the result is music that's as honest as he knows how to make.

"Making art is about telling the truth, and making people feel more human and less alone. Sometimes Peter does that," says Mulvey's Redbird bandmate Jeffrey Foucault. "He's a good storyteller, he's funny as hell, and he wants to deliver every night. He works hard to make a connection with people, and pays attention to craft. He's a pro."

Delmhorst, meanwhile, admires Mulvey's commitment to being truly present for each show, and adds that she enjoys his refreshments: "As a performer, he stays present in the room — you won't often see him curl into himself or phone it in. He shows up for the audience whether or not he's feeling it 100 percent at that moment or not. He also has a limitless supply of snacks on his person at any given time, and makes lovely little thermoses of Manhattans, so all in all

he's someone you want on your team."

Hearing those musings on Mulvey's hard work and generous sharing of snacks and booze, one can't help but trace the arc of his life and career. After all, this kid from Milwaukee's Sherman Park neighborhood was born to international volunteers. This child growing up white on a predominantly black playground in a very segregated city. This seven-year-old seeing his camp counselor play guitar and knowing that's what he wants to do

with his life. All of that — all the time — catapulted Mulvey toward the music he now makes.

And somewhere in this reverie, Mulvey is singing his song "Wings of the Ragman":

Back in your old yard,
the tree from your childhood
Is thinking about you,
and shivers a sigh
And it's all around you now. ■

Downtown Milwaukee

Gary Clark Jr. at Antone's in Austin.

MY TALE OF TWO CITIES

The interwoven worlds of Austin and Chicago

by Don McLeese

> **"Austin audiences and Chicago audiences can both smell a phony right off the bat. And Chicago recognizes that Austin bands, in general, are playing because they enjoy it."**
>
> Max Crawford (Poi Dog Pondering)

IT WAS THE SORT OF EVENING I'd learned to enjoy so much in Austin and had rarely experienced anywhere else: A group of great musicians coming together to celebrate one of their own.

Austin is, after all, known for things like a "Hoot Night" of Beatles vs. Stones at the Hole in the Wall or a birthday tribute to Townes Van Zandt at the Cactus Café. Most memorably, at the closing of Liberty Lunch, there was a marathon performance of "Gloria," with Van the Man himself even phoning in to join the proceedings. The spirit of such gatherings is always communal, shared among musicians and fans alike. There's something present you can't replicate, can't bottle and sell, can't save for posterity. These particular musicians will never again play these particular songs in these particular configurations. It's a way of coming together and even of giving back. There's little or no money in it for anyone, except maybe the beer sales that might help pay the rent. It's one night only. If you weren't there, you missed it.

On the night in question, I wasn't in Austin. I was at the Hideout in Chicago, which looked like Austin incarnate: another working-class, shot-and-a-beer joint. Strings of white Christmas lights illuminated the low ceiling, even though we were still weeks from Halloween.

The Hideout is in a nondescript part of town, not even a neighborhood, really, just a side street off a diagonal street that can make finding it a challenge. You wouldn't happen by or stumble in. You would have to know where you were going. Yet the place was packed on a Monday night, ready to celebrate the music of T Bone Burnett, a Texas treasure long before he became a national one. It was the Chicago launch for the first book that's been written about Burnett, a musical biography by my great friend and longtime colleague Lloyd Sachs, titled *T Bone Burnett: A Life in Pursuit,* published by the Austin-based University of Texas Press.

The musical part of the evening featured members of two beloved local bands — one of whom, Kelly Hogan, used to support herself tending bar at this very club. Hogan and Nora O' Connor — who share vocals in Chicago's Flat Five and have backed other acts as variant as the Decemberists and former Austin resident Alejandro Escovedo — were fronting the tribute band with guitarist Steve Dawson, the ace singer-songwriter from Chicago band Dolly Varden. The rhythm section was drummer Gerald Dowd and bassist John Abbey, not members of either band, but in Chicago (like in Austin) everybody plays with everybody.

It was a night of revelation, featuring performances of relative obscurities — not the best-known songs from Burnett's breakthrough production of *O Brother, Where Art Thou?* or the *Raising Sand* team-up of bluegrass fiddler/singer Alison Krauss and former Led Zeppelin frontman Robert Plant (who lived in Austin for a time). Burnett is known for blurring musical categories and transcending them, and Austin is known for that as well. That town brings together musicians you wouldn't think necessarily belong together, generating a dynamic that defies preconception.

The Flat Five

And this night's show all the way in Chicago was built upon that same dynamic: One night only, never to be repeated.

No Pretense, No Problem

I lived and worked in Austin throughout the 1990s. In Chicago — which was my hometown for the first 40 years of my life, though I moved away a quarter-century ago — I see a city that has somehow begun to channel more and more of the musical spirit of Austin. It might be a stretch to call them sister cities, but there is a strong musical kinship that keeps getting stronger.

That kinship cuts to the heart of the heartland. Both Austin and Chicago have their own cachet, but they're both far from the coasts, where the cultural arbiters and industries consolidate and the trends generate. Both cities have long been suspicious of those trends, preferring that the roots of their culture remain deep and "authentic" (a problematic term, but one on which we

can likely agree here in terms of meaning — or at least Chicago and Austin can).

Both take a certain pride in a strong work ethic, despite Austin's former reputation as Slacker Central. And both are suspicious of pretty boys and prima donnas.

"There's something in common between Austin and Chicago, and that is a total lack of tolerance for pretension," multi-instrumentalist Max Crawford told me a couple decades ago, shortly after relocating as a member of Poi Dog Pondering from Austin to Chicago, where he is now as much a fixture as he had been in Austin when I'd met him.

"Austin audiences and Chicago audiences can both smell a phony right off the bat," he continued. "And Chicago recognizes that Austin bands, in general, are playing because they enjoy it."

Both cities harbor something of a grudge against the music industry for ignoring or not properly marketing their music. Though, fact is, both depend on the live dynamic — the interaction of

artist and audience — that is so hard to transfer to the recording studio. You take the music out of either of these towns, and you've got something different.

That is, unless you take Chicago to Austin — witness the annual Bloodshot Records South by Southwest blowout at Austin's Yard Dog gallery. Or take Austin to Chicago — as Poi Dog Pondering, one of Austin's most popular bands, discovered when it transplanted itself to Chicago. There, the group became something different and better, and one of Chicago's most popular bands.

Once upon a time, you could hear this musical exchange over the airwaves, with KGSR in Austin and WXRT in Chicago both enjoying national reputations as unique stations that represented their respected cities and reflected them in ways that more tightly formatted stations could not.

You could feel the common musical denominator on the night in question in Chicago, at the Hideout, where vocalist extraordinaire Kelly Hogan launched a

Austin, Texas

residency that was much like the Tuesday "Hippie Hour" with Toni Price that packed Austin's Continental Club in the '90s (and that has since returned). In fact, the Hideout could have easily been picked up and set down in Austin, where I'm told its owners frequently visit, where so many of the artists and those who run and patronize the club have developed strong ties to SXSW.

The T Bone Burnett tribute notwithstanding, Monday night at the Hideout typically finds the mercurial Robbie Fulks and a rotating cast of guests staging what could just as easily be called "Hoot Night." Just like at Austin's Hole in the Wall, there is a different theme every week. One memorable night was billed as "Lynyrd Skynyrd vs. Leonard Cohen," an evening of mix-and-match material from two very different songbooks (and artists with two very different audiences). Another featured the Reeds: Jerry vs. Lou.

Opening the Pipeline

The real home for Austin in Chicago will forever be FitzGerald's, the first club to present so many of the Austin artists who now consider Chicago one of their strongest markets. I've long praised the venue — which used to be known as the Deer Lodge — as my favorite Texas roadhouse. It has somehow sustained itself in decidedly unfashionable Berywn, just south of Ernest Hemingway's Oak Park and not far from Al Capone's Cicero. Yet stepping into FitzGerald's for a night of music with Joe Ely or Alejandro Escovedo — or even Los Lobos — is like entering not only a timewarp but also a spacewarp, where you know this music belongs and so do you.

FitzGerald's is the first and the best of the area clubs to bring that Texas roadhouse spirit up north, sparking this Chicago-Austin synergy shortly after opening in 1980. Owner Bill FitzGerald,

Ball subsequently convinced many of her fellow Austin musicians that this homey place in a blue-collar suburb was the real deal, opening a pipeline for acts from Texas and Louisiana to head north. One was a skinny guitarist named Stevie Ray Vaughan, without a record deal, who tore the place up. (Chicago's Alligator Records decided to pass on him; at the time, it wasn't interested in white guys playing his brand of blues.)

FitzGerald's made an even bigger splash when it brought zydeco kingpin Clifton Chenier north for his first area appearance in decades, an engagement that led to long lines outside the club and drew TV news cameras. Chenier subsequently made FitzGerald's a regular stop on his touring schedule.

For decades, FitzGerald's American Music Festival around the Fourth of July has ranked among the best celebrations in the country for roots music in general and Austin music in particular. Ball has a standing invitation, and other Austin artists such as Ely, Escovedo, and Jon Dee Graham — all promoted to Chicago audiences by the family-run club — have made this a home away from home. FitzGerald and his wife, Kate, have continued to make it feel like home for everyone who comes there or plays there.

It has certainly been a special stop for Ely, who once played a memorable New Year's Eve gig in Berwyn, instead of where you'd expect to find him in Austin or Lubbock. Chicago's Vlasta the Polka Queen serenaded the crowd with "Auld Lang Syne" before Ely and band stormed the stage. Ely had been booking multiple nights at the club since his lineup paired guitarist David Grissom with saxophonist Bobby Keys, and those who heard that then-unrecorded band there will never forget it. (Those who didn't can hear it on Ely's archival *Live Chicago* 1987 album.)

As Grissom told me again when I worked in Austin, "There were nights at FitzGerald's where it was like, this is it, man; it does not get any better than this."

When Alejandro Escovedo had his near-death collapse from hepatitis in 2003, his first live performance following his recovery was at FitzGerald's, before he even committed to any Texas dates. His band featured Graham, in a reunion of the two True Believers. Now Graham returns to FitzGerald's so often it seems as much his home club as does the Continental in Austin, where he generally plays two nights a week when he's off the road.

"I've got two nightclub homes: the Continental in Austin and FitzGerald's in Berwyn, period," agreed Graham. "They get what it is I do [at FitzGerald's], and they've treated me well since my first show there."

I was a western suburbanite who loved the rootsier music FitzGerald's was bringing to town long before there was any sort of alt-country bandwagon. When I wasn't writing about music for work at the *Chicago Sun-Times*, I was often listening to music at FitzGerald's — and writing about it — for fun. Bill FitzGerald was just about the only person bringing this music to town, and I was one of the few writing about it. And I would meet my friends John Soss and Lloyd Sachs there regularly, marveling at the intensity of this music that still seemed like a cult passion within Chicago at large.

By 1985, FitzGerald's was so much like home that when my wife Maria and I got married, we had our reception there — the first one that FitzGerald's had ever hosted. We even picked a church in Berwyn, one that would accommodate my Catholic bride and her divorced fiancé, just for its proximity to the club. It was the classiest little honky-tonk soiree you could ever imagine in the suburbs of Chicago.

Soon, other clubs started following FitzGerald's lead in booking hard-rocking fare with country roots. This wasn't the hippie-dippy "country-rock" reheated from the '70s, but a stronger strain with some punk-rock attitude to match its honky-tonk spirit. Soon we'd be hearing more of it at SXSW, and soon

a huge music fan with no experience running a club, decided to venture beyond the local talent pool and called Austinite Marcia Ball as his first national act to play his new place.

"I thought, what does Chicago need with a white girl who plays the blues?" Ball told me when I was living in Austin and working for the paper there. "But not only did we make fans up here, we made friends. I'd take these people on the road with me. You're in the home of the blues — the north end of the whole blues spectrum, where so much of it was born and recorded. And these people have got a pride about it, and are just as soulful as they can be."

after that I moved from Chicago to Austin, drawn by the siren song of this music.

Chicago Blues Down South

I can't go much further into this story without invoking the name of the late, great Doug Sahm, whose booking at FitzGerald's toward the end of the 1980s helped pave my path to Austin. Or at least that's what Sahm long claimed. It's a convoluted story, like every story of Sahm's was.

After the musical baptism I'd received at FitzGerald's, I had been following my passion to its Texas source pretty much since the beginning of South by Southwest. The cheap Mexican food, temperate March climate, and relaxed atmosphere had made this spring break for the music industry, and my favorite reporting assignment of the year. (It was also a chance for club owners like FitzGerald, who had already been making spring pilgrimages to Jazzfest in New Orleans, to discover plenty more Texas talent worth bringing north.)

One particularly memorable SXSW evening found Sahm playing at a club called Antone's, which I had come to consider the quintessential Chicago blues bar, even though it was a thousand miles south.

Clifford Antone loved the music and the musicians so much that he'd pretty much adopt a guy like the late Hubert Sumlin (the great guitarist for Howlin' Wolf) or pianist Pinetop Perkins (from the Muddy Waters band), give them a home to live in and a place to play, and treat them like the musical royalty he knew they were. And when Chicago bluesmen would play Austin, they'd get the crack Antone's house band behind them and a knowledgeable, passionate audience that wouldn't be content with them sleepwalking through "Sweet Home Chicago" or going through the generic motions that might satisfy the

tourists up north. No, in Austin, the musicians and fans forced the artists to dig deep and play with fire.

The blues crackled at Antone's, and the Texas audience responded to Chicago music at this club as rapturously as the Chicago crowd responded to Austin music at FitzGerald's.

What made it all come together on this particular SXSW evening was that Sahm's West Side Horns had been hassled by the police for smoking pot in the Antone's parking lot. Thus, they were indisposed to come to the stage for the showcase. Stepping in to substitute was Kim Wilson, frontman and harmonica ace for the Fabulous Thunderbirds, an Austin-based band steeped in the blues of Chicago. The result was another of those "only in Austin" experiences — if you weren't there, you missed it — with Sahm's singing and playing pure Texas, Wilson's harp pure Chicago, and the combination pure magic.

Before FitzGerald's lured Sahm to make his long overdue debut at the club, I flew back to Austin for an interview with Sahm and Antone. We bonded as much over baseball — my beloved Cubs, Antone's Yankees, Sahm's passion and baseball knowledge as deep as any sports fanatic I've ever met — and over Chicago, which Antone loved for its music and Sahm knew well from the days when he was on Mercury Records, which had been based there.

When I subsequently made the move a few months later from the *Sun-Times* to the *Austin American-Statesman* — one that Sahm insisted he had suggested and inspired — many of my Chicago colleagues thought I was nuts. Nobody moved willingly from a big-market paper to a medium-market one, but I'd spent enough time in Austin to know that I could feel as at home there as I did at FitzGerald's. I'd talked enough blues and baseball with Sahm and Antone to know I'd find kindred spirits there, and I had eaten at enough

Mexican restaurants during SXSW to realize I'd never go hungry.

Insurgent Country

So Austin took me in and made me feel at home like no place could, other than Chicago. Chicago may have been a bigger and tougher city, but more and more Austin musicians were finding receptive audiences and spirited receptions up there, while more and more Chicagoans were making annual pilgrimages to SXSW, sharing the magic, spreading the word.

It was after my family moved to Austin in 1990 that the synergy with Chicago really surged back home, the influence and the energy flowing both ways. SXSW had a lot to do with promoting this cultural exchange, as it had with me. Having FitzGerald's already in place as a northern outpost

"I thought, what does Chicago need with a white girl who plays the blues? But not only did we make fans up here, we made friends. I'd take these people on the road with me."
Marcia Ball

Chicago

for this music was crucial, and both the music and the audience were spreading to bigger venues as well.

Before leaving Chicago, I had written a Sunday *Sun-Times* arts cover story linking Ely, Steve Earle, and Dwight Yoakam under some sort of neotraditionalist banner. Chicago was becoming one of the best markets even for those outside Austin who mined that seam between rock and country. It wasn't "country-rock," and it didn't seem to be just another fashion statement. It was tougher, rootsier, more indigenous — all qualities Austin generated and Chicago deeply respected.

Whatever this music was, its most aggressive offshoot seemed equally reflective of punk attitude and a reverence for country tradition as an antidote to modern plasticity. That strain started deepening its roots in

Chicago's soil, most significantly through the emergence of Bloodshot Records and its "insurgent country" catalog. Just as FitzGerald's is my favorite Texas roadhouse and Antone's is the best Chicago blues bar, Bloodshot is the best Austin label, though it happens to be based in Chicago. Not only did Alejandro Escovedo's stepping-stone stint with the label produce some of his best music, but it raised the Chicago label's profile in Austin in general and SXSW in particular.

"It certainly gave us more credibility in Austin," said Nan Warshaw, co-owner of Bloodshot. "He played that closing night at South by Southwest at La Zona Rosa, and the place was packed. When he said how happy he was to be on Bloodshot, it brought tears to our eyes.

"There's something about the Central time zone," she adds. "There's this path up and down."

Ryan Adams and the Old 97's are among the acts that released music on Bloodshot early in their careers. The label still has Texans Scott Biram, Rosie Flores, and Wayne Hancock on its roster. But its flagship star is plainly Jon Langford, the Welshman from seminal punk band the Mekons, who transplanted himself to Chicago after I'd left and has made his music all but synonymous with that of Bloodshot Records.

It was in Chicago that Langford formed the mighty Waco Brothers, a name inspired by the Texas town just 100 miles north of Austin. In the process, he provided another one of those expansive bridges between Chicago and Austin. He has been earning renown through his side career as a respected visual artist, and his home gallery is Austin's Yard Dog.

In what has become one of the liveliest traditions of South by

Southwest, Yard Dog hosts an annual Bloodshot bash during one festival afternoon. The same spirit that flourishes at FitzGerald's throughout the American Music Festival turns the art gallery into a free-for-all during SXSW, when Chicago invades Austin.

Just as Bloodshot brings Chicago to Austin each spring, Yard Dog recently made its own reciprocal visit to Chicago, where the city's Firecat Gallery presented a Yard Dog show devoted to Langford and another of the Austin gallery's popular musical-visual artists, Bob Schneider.

But the artists who best embody the synergy for me are the ones who moved with Frank Orrall in the early 1990s to transplant the core of Poi Dog Pondering from Austin to Chicago, transforming the band's music in the process.

The band still features Max Crawford and violinist Susan Voelz, who had been Poi Dog mainstays in Austin and then Chicago. Voelz also tours with Escovedo when Poi Dog has down time, and recently released *Beautiful Life: Songs of Prince Re-Imagined,* a tribute album recorded over two decades in both Austin and Chicago.

Crawford has even gotten a job with my beloved Chicago Cubs, manning the video board. He also played on the recently released debut album by Hogan and O'Connor's the Flat Five, *It's a World of Love and Hope.* (Of course he did.) He also bartends at Metro, long one of the city's premier rock bars, across the street from Wrigley Field, and has for 24 years.

"I didn't really plan on staying," said Crawford, who has now lived in Chicago almost as long as I've been gone. "I just wanted to live in a big city, and this seemed very livable. The musicians are very supportive of each other, just like they were in Austin. Because both cities

Alejandro Escovedo
at FitzGerald's in Chicago.

are so removed from the music industry. Everybody's got a day job — unless you're [Wilco's] Jeff Tweedy. People play for the joy of it here."

Creative Connections

I could write at length about all sorts of other pipeline connections: How members of punk-rock's Scratch Acid moved from Austin to Chicago and morphed into the Jesus Lizard. How Lollapalooza reinvented itself from a touring festival into an annual Chicago event, produced by Austin's C3 Presents. How those same producers — known to friends in Austin as "the three Charlies" — then brought that concept back home when they launched the Austin City Limits festival. How *Austin City Limits* itself was preceded on public television by Chicago's *Soundstage*, which originated in 1972 as *Made in Chicago*.

Perhaps the most enviable itinerary is that of publicist Heather West, who hit the trifecta. She left her hometown of Austin, spent a decade in New Orleans, then moved to Chicago. She initially did some work for Bloodshot and now has a full slate of clients, including the Riot Fest every summer.

"My first trips to Chicago were to work with Jimmy Rogers on his album releases for Antone's," remembers West. "It happened to coincide with the period where folks from Austin were moving to Chicago — from David Yow, David Sims, and Duane Denison heading up and starting Jesus Lizard to folks like Debbie Pastor [longtime Austin scenester and member of the crew from the 1991 film *Slacker*] going up and working on music and film projects.

"It kinda hit my radar screen," she adds, "and I realized that while Chicago certainly has well-defined scenes, there is also a sense of community that is undeniable. ... I always loved [the judgment-free scenes] in Austin. Growing up I went to see rock, punk, blues, whatever and never felt out of place at anything.

"You saw it back then in [Chicago's] Wicker Park, among all the creative people, between social bonds and incestuous relationships, as well as the gathering en masse that happened when someone was in need."

One Night Only

To bring this story full circle, I had never heard of drummer Gerald Dowd before the release party at the Hideout for Lloyd Sachs' book on T Bone Burnett. Then I saw him open for Ian Hunter at City Winery a few days later, no drums in sight, just him and the better-known Robbie Fulks providing guitar and high harmonies in support.

I learned that he had two self-released CDs, and that the first, an EP, had a majestic cover of the Charlie Rich ballad, "Life's Little Ups and Downs," written by Rich's wife, Margaret Ann, and one of my favorite cuts ever. It's the kind of music I'd learned to love even more deeply in Austin.

If that introduction didn't sound already enough like what I'd expect from an Austin artist, a little research confirmed it. I learned that the guy had been dubbed "the hardest-working drummer in Chicago," had played with pretty much everyone. He had staged a charity event at FitzGerald's a year earlier, launching his full-length album debut, all proceeds benefitting the Chicago Greater Food Depository.

It was billed as "Day of the Dowd," in reference to "Day of the Dead," the Mexican holiday honoring the deceased — a tradition that had once been far more prominent in Austin than in Chicago. No more, thanks to the National Museum of Mexican Art, a wonderful institution in Chicago's Pilsen neighborhood, which marks the holiday with an extended celebration.

The evening at FitzGerald's, maybe a 20-minute drive from that Mexican neighborhood of Pilsen, promised "16 bands. 13 hours. ONE drummer." One night only, it goes without saying. If you weren't there, you missed it.

And since Kelly Hogan and Nora O'Connor were both among the listed luminaries, perhaps all of the musicians — and much of the crowd — that I saw at the Hideout book bash had been at the FitzGerald's extravaganza as well.

That's what community is all about, that sharing and that giving. And that's what I had found in Austin, the land of a thousand musical benefits, where "friends with benefits" has a whole different meaning. Where musicians show up for these events not to make money, but to raise it, just as Dowd and friends had. If you're a musician in Austin, you play benefits with your friends, often and happily, because you know (or at least hope) the whole community will rally around you when you need it.

One of the latest and greatest examples of such rallying is the fund for Austin's George Reiff, whose cancer has threatened his life as well as his livelihood. As with Gerald Dowd in Chicago, everyone in the musical community of Austin knows Reiff, not only as a bassist and producer, but as a great guy, and the sort of musician who makes every band he is in better.

A GoFundMe campaign to help cover Reiff's treatment, recovery and lost income has raised more than $125,000 of its $200,000 goal. Pretty much every week my Facebook feed shows another benefit for George — a different club, a different bill of acts, filled with musicians who love him and just can't do enough for him, and drawing fans who are friends who feel the same.

That was the spirit that I once moved from Chicago to Austin to discover, that sense of musical community, that feeling of playing music mostly for the love of it, for the hell of it, for the sense that this experience wasn't a product that could be packaged and marketed and sold, but something to be shared for one night only. A quarter-century ago, I felt that what I had discovered — that spirit of musical community and connection — was exclusively Austin's. But, now, when I return to Chicago, I see it there as well. Only in Austin, and only in Chicago. ∎

Making It in the Middle

by Allison Moorer

"I TOLD YOU NOT TO BOOK Cleveland," I said through clenched teeth.

I was on the phone with my manager, heading southeast from Ann Arbor, where I'd played the night before. We were conducting our daily postmortem — analyzing the previous night's successes and failures and discussing what was ahead. Seconds after he gave me the latest ticket count for Cleveland's Beachland Ballroom, that evening's venue, I felt the heat of embarrassment and anger rise from my chest and spread to the tips of my ears. I'd had maybe my worst road experience there the year before when, if memory serves, I sold 22 tickets.

I was adamant about not repeating what had felt like a debacle. I'd told my manager and booking agent to please go around Cleveland when they booked the duo tour I was doing to keep a presence on the road between albums and to maybe make a little money. Neither of them listened.

"Cancel Cleveland," I said over and over.

They didn't.

"The promoter thinks things will go better this time."

"It's a slow build."

But I didn't want to go to Cleveland. And it looked like Cleveland didn't want me to come. That morning's numbers revealed hardly any increase from the previous year's, and the promoter wanted to cut my guarantee in half but otherwise hold me to my contract.

I sarcastically told my manager I appreciated his listening to me, then told him to tell the promoter to perform some unsavory act on himself. Then I pointed the van toward Columbus for a much-needed night off.

I spent that evening in bed, reading a handful of angry messages from fans who'd bought tickets for the show on my website message board.

They were right to be angry. I shouldn't have canceled. I should've gone to Cleveland and played for whomever came, for whatever money I could get. I should've gotten up and tried again, ticket counts be damned. You can't afford to have pride in this business, even if it keeps you from losing money. If you don't show up for your fans, no matter how many of them there are, they'll stop showing up for you.

The truth is that the Midwest is hard to crack, and I was frustrated — I was doing pretty well on the coasts and didn't understand why I was having such a hard time between them. I studied my Soundscan numbers and my ticket counts. New York City? Great. Los Angeles? Better. Seattle? Portland? Terrific. Austin? Texas is always good. Even college towns were pretty decent. The press was on board from my very first single. I was a bona fide critic's darling.

But guess who didn't know I existed? Any audience that relied on radio to find music. The program directors at the big heartland radio stations didn't get me. They didn't care that I'd had a song in a Robert Redford movie and had received an Oscar nomination for it — in fact, they seemed to resent it. They didn't care that I'd been covered in *Interview Magazine* and had been on *The Tonight Show* and *David Letterman* (hardly any country acts scored those kinds of things). And it seemed they decided because I had, I wasn't part of their club and was some sort of propped-up, pampered Hollywood act.

I wasn't, but I failed to make sure they knew it.

Mainstream radio wouldn't touch me. I couldn't draw flies in the markets they controlled. If CMT hadn't played my videos, I probably wouldn't have sold even those 22 tickets in Cleveland in August of 2002.

I clung to the sides of the country like it was a swimming pool and I couldn't do anything but dog paddle a little if I let go — which was true. I couldn't connect with the folks who didn't get my artsy Gram Parsons references or understand why I never took the mic off the stand to "work" the stage. Without radio, I remained undiscovered by people who didn't know where to go to discover music that was considered too edgy for the middle of the dial. I don't think there was anything I could've done to change my fate there. I wasn't producing the kind of music they seemed to want to play, had no intention to, and I'd struck out so many times there was no way they'd have touched me even if I had. I was left with the two choices any artist without a hit has — work harder and make fans one by one, by returning to markets over and over again, or give up. I chose the latter, not realizing the long-term investment I wasn't making.

It's easy to get caught up in the hype, to believe that because you can draw in areas that are full of people who seek the unique that you don't need anything else. But you do need something else if you want a solid career. You can't get by on fickle tastemaker turnout for long. Los Angeles might be sexier than Des Moines, but at the end of the day you need the lover *and* the friend. The discoverers always move on to the next discovery. I didn't know that. In all my newcomer's hubris, I thought I could stay in the game without the core. Bad move. The middle gives you staying power.

Tennessee Williams said, "America has only three cities: New York, San Francisco, and New Orleans. Everywhere else is Cleveland." But Cleveland still counts, and everywhere else does too. Given another chance at that morning, I'd go back and drive there no matter what my manager told me. I'd go over and over until I'd built an audience who knew they could count on me.

As Ohio goes, so goes the nation. ∎

Three Brothers Farm in Wisconsin.

FILL THE ROOM

Peeking in on the Upper Midwest's music venues

by Kevin Lynch

PEOPLE MOST FREQUENTLY think of the Upper Midwest as being blanketed with several varieties of beautiful landscapes, from solemn mounds built ages ago by indigenous people to the verdant valleys immortalized by painters John Steuart Curry and Grant Wood. Hamlets and towns lie amid the great hills of Wisconsin's Kettle Moraine and the southern regions of Wisconsin and Minnesota. Some call that area "God's Country," others call it the heartland — it's ever-changing, derived from the same glacial flow that shaped the Great Lakes. But look closer into those landscapes and you will find more than just pretty scenery: the Upper Midwest has plenty to offer the ears, too, in the form of some great venues for live roots music.

Some Midwest venues are bars and theaters nestled into small towns or big-city neighborhoods, others — the barns, basements, and outside shows — are more out-of-the-way. As restless American wanderer Herman Melville said, some of the best rooms are "not on any map; true places never are." Yet regional audiences and appreciative touring troubadours have found them.

Open-Handed Spirit

The weather in the Upper Midwest is a capricious force — a placid, leafy hypnotizer one moment, and just as quickly a snarling demon. Close to the highway, our wind blasts against shuddering, rusty-nailed boards, time-stained windows, and shingle-flapping roofs. But drive off the road, into the country, and the wind settles.

In one such place, Three Brothers Farm stands amid rolling pastures not far from the sumptuous hills of Kettle Moraine State Forest, the town of Merton, and Oconomowoc, Wisconsin. The farm's music performance barn sits atop a hill. The breeze whistles softly through the space, then back out to the

Three Brothers Farm

wide-open chicken-grazing yard and corn fields beyond — all perfectly framed through an open barn door to the left of the stage. A gust outside might cause one of the old farm tools hanging on the walls to swing slightly, as if responding to a musical rhythm.

On one recent evening, veteran Texas singer-songwriter and storyteller Eric Taylor was tuning up in the barn. He has toured around the world, but this place is something else. He says it's one of the most beautiful places he's ever played. His music and storytelling take their sweet time, and his music sounds as comfortable as old boots, but with curious creases and twists, sometimes a tough leather toe in the gut.

There's nothing more redolent of American roots culture than hearing an acoustic performer — like Taylor or Catlin Canty, Jeffrey Foucault, Whitney Mann, Josh Harty, the double-banjo duo the Lowest Pair, or the Madison singer-songwriter couple Count This Penny — in the barn of a functioning community-supported agriculture (CSA) farm.

When it's not presenting music, Three Brothers Farm raises 1,200 nesting hens for eggs to sell to southeast Wisconsin markets. This organic farming reaches back to the tough-yet-pastoral time before modern factory agriculture. Of course the music, with its lyrical tangles and idiosyncratic refrains, feels just as organic.

Three Brothers became a music venue when one of the brothers, Michael Gutschenritter, saw an open inquiry on Jeffrey Foucault's blog: A Wisconsin native, the singer-songwriter wondered if anyone had a barn in Wisconsin where he could perform. The brothers had an extra barn they were, at the time, using mainly for storage.

"I called Jeffrey's agent and we had a booking within an hour," Gutschenritter recalls. Sometimes things come together like a hitch to a ready plow. It sure clicked for Foucault, who now lives in western Massachusetts and

relentlessly searches for the perfect venue.

"Three Brothers Farm is about the best thing of its kind that I've seen or played," Foucault says. "A beautiful old barn on a working farm was turned, with some thought and care, into a real intimate venue that outshines most clubs in its attention to detail: good sound and light, good food, and an open-handed spirit. It feels real because it is real. If they tried the same thing on either of the coasts there's a good chance it would suffer from a self-conscious sense of irony. ... But not in Oconomowoc, Wisconsin."

A basic premise in the still-hard daily life of a farm is that "we need to put all available space to use," Gutschenritter says. The barn is used now for about four artist events each summer. "We try not to do too many concerts because we want each one to be special," he adds.

On concert night you show up to see smoke rising from homemade pizzas

that bake in a stone oven at the bottom of the grassy hill. You can order wine, beer, and other beverages. A few old couches and a motley variety of wooden chairs and tables litter the barn, all focused on the stage. Before each set, Michael Gutschenritter gives an opening spiel explaining the farm's history, functions, and ideals. From there, it's all about the music.

"I'd play Three Brothers Farm solely for the kind hospitality of the Gutschenritter family," says fast-ascending troubadour Caitlin Canty. "Add the gorgeous setting and fresh homemade food ... playing wooden instruments in wooden rooms feels and sounds right."

The Midwest has other music barns too, including Codfish Hollow near Maquoketa, Iowa, set in a picturesque glen, with hayrack rides from the parking lot to the barn. By contrast, the Shitty Barn in Spring Green, Wisconsin, is a weather-worn red barn situated in

"A beautiful old barn on a working farm was turned, with some thought and care, into a real intimate venue that outshines most clubs in its attention to detail: good sound and light, good food, and an open-handed spirit. It feels real because it is real. If they tried the same thing on either of the coasts there's a good chance it would suffer from a self-conscious sense of irony."

Jeffrey Foucault

less-than-idyllic environs in an industrial park. The ceiling hovers low in a cozy, wood-beamed space. A rising garage door behind the stage allows for a leafy backdrop. The catered food is classy, organic, and fresh. Spring Green is just north of the Wisconsin River and near Frank Lloyd Wright's historic home Taliesin, conceived as an interface between human design and nature.

There's also the outlying Barn at LaGrange, located between East Troy, Wisconsin — site of the huge outdoor concert venue Alpine Valley Music Theater — and Whitewater on Highway 20. The Barn at LaGrange bills itself as a house concert and attendance is by invitation only. It has a flower-bedecked, knotty-wooded charm, but seating is formal proscenium-style.

These very worthy places have longer track records, but for my money, none possesses Three Brothers' breeze-blessed, lost-in-time aura.

Spreading Roots

In Michigan, the most notable performance spaces are the more conventional kind. The Ark in Ann Arbor and the Eccentric Café at Bell's Brewery in Kalamazoo serve the greater acoustic world. Flint has the Sippin' Lizard Coffee House, and Grand Rapids has the Rosa Parks Circle downtown. Named for the civil rights activist who lived out her days in Michigan, it was designed by Maya Lin, famous for designing the Vietnam War Memorial.

Davenport, Iowa, throws the Mississippi Valley Blues Festival, located at the great river's convergence of ports,

the Quad Cities, on the river shore. Traditionally the event has been held on Independence Day weekend, complete with fireworks over the river. Even if you're hounded by the deepest imaginable woes, hearing the blues played out in the grit, grass, and sky of a heartland crossroads seems to chase that devil away.

Minnesota, meanwhile, is brimming with clubs like Bo Diddley's Pub and Deli in St. Cloud, the Gingko Coffee House in St. Paul, and the Fine Line Music Café in Minneapolis. Of course there's also St. Paul's Fitzgerald Theater — home of the long-exalted *A Prairie Home Companion* public radio show first hosted by Garrison Keillor, and now by mandolin virtuoso Chris Thile. There's a Midwestern event if there ever was one.

However, the real musical heart of the heartland may be the Homestead Pickin' Parlor in Richfield, which bills itself as "The Home of Twin Cities Folk Music since 1979." It has long dedicated itself to the development of a roots music community via formal instrument instruction, workshops, and sales of instruments, musician accessories, and obscure acoustic-music recordings. Though there are certainly venues throughout the continental US — and the world — that provide a sort of one-stop shop for the surrounding music community, the Pickin' Parlor's confluence of high-quality performance, instruction, recording archives, and other music community-building ventures is truly characteristic of the Midwest.

In Chicago — perhaps the region's most famous music town — another such center is at the Old Town School of Folk Music, which opened in 1957 and

remains the nation's most dedicated space for folk music. The midcity venue showcased early folk-blues-gospel pioneers like Pete Seeger, Mahalia Jackson, and Big Bill Broonzy, and later nurtured the great Chicagoans John Prine, Steve Goodman, Bonnie Koloc, and Roger McGuinn of The Byrds. Old Town grew from its cultural roots up, as an alternative music education and performance institution. Like other important Chicago blues and jazz venues, Old Town helped pull Southern roots culture northward.

In 1998, Joni Mitchell and Peter Yarrow (of Peter, Paul and Mary) helped fund the venue's move and renovation in its present home, a converted public library. It's a fitting space considering the encyclopedic approach the school embraces. The new digs include fully equipped contemporary music classrooms warmed by Oriental rugs and offers instruction in many folk instruments and virtually all vernaculars of American music, including electric rock and roll. Wander further inside and you'll find a rehearsal and sing-along space with piano; a dance studio; a music store that sells, rents, and repairs acoustic instruments; and the Resource Center, an extensive recording archive of CDs, LPs, and 78s that's run by affable folklorist and fiddler Paul Tyler. You see the future of American roots music in a youth-oriented chamber performance space with murals celebrating music and nature, a juice bar, children's concerts, and a monthly open-mic night for teens.

Old Town's main performance space, Maurer Hall, has a thrust stage and a combination of cabaret and bench

Old Town School's Maurer Hall in Chicago.

seating on two levels. An open area in front of the stage allows for folk dancing. Since Chicago is the crossroads of the Midwest, the programming is more cosmopolitan than old-timey, with plenty of world music and family programs amid a wide array of American roots artists — many of them innovators.

A newer venue, SPACE (The Society for the Preservation of Arts and Culture in Evanston), is tucked behind Union Pizzeria in downtown Evanston, Illinois. It's a nightclub that draws blues, jazz, and other top roots music acts with high-tech sound and fine acoustics under an arched wooden ceiling.

Four overhanging lamps with exotic fabric shades that resemble the undersides of giant mushrooms softly illuminate before and between sets. The purple, translucent curtain behind the stage adds more "spacey" atmosphere that lets you feel you've escaped the rat race, at least for a few hours.

Other roots and folk music spaces speckle the greater Chicago area, including the Acorn Coffeehouse in Wheaton and the somewhat peripatetic Off Square Music organization in Woodstock, Illinois, where the town square was made famous by the movie

Groundhog Day.

More than Brew City

Back in the Badger State, a well-intentioned roots music fan would do well visiting Milwaukee. For starters, it is a very easy large city to navigate, making it easy to find gems like Linneman's Riverwest Inn situated in the city's old, hip Riverwest neighborhood.

From outside, the 1902 building stands big-shouldered and shadow-haunted. Linneman's Inn dominates a corner close to the Milwaukee River, on a block deeply invested in Americana. For example, on the next corner is Ma Baensch's marinated herring factory, which has churned out jars of wild-caught herring, a Midwest holiday favorite, since 1932.

Once inside Linneman's, the tone and mood shifts. The bar resembles many classic Brew City pubs, except for big Bob Dylan and John Lennon posters. Inn owner Jim Linneman's longtime partner, known only as Marty, tends bar with smiling grace. A substantial back performance room includes a generous stage and a hulking, peculiarly alluring chair near the women's restroom carved

completely out of a tree trunk of "overgrown boxelder," Linneman says.

Then there's the closet space at the back of the listening room. Jammed inside is a sophisticated soundboard attached to one inner closet wall, barely leaving room for a small chair. Linneman must be part spelunker or mad scientist: he spends most of each performance crammed inside this hole, like a standing casket wired to musical lightning, a touch of Gothic matching the venue's brooding exterior. Seated sideways from the stage, he helps coax the music to sharp, vivid life. "I've been coming out of the closet for years," he jokes.

"We really care about the music," he adds. "This is not about business. I'm not much of a businessman. My partner and I are music lovers and people lovers."

Besides hosting a stream of traveling troubadours and bands, this stage has been frequented by local and regional stars including Minneapolis country-blues hound Charlie Parr, Milwaukee R&B king Paul Cebar, all three members of the iconic rock trio Violent Femmes, and perhaps Milwaukee's most popular roots-rock band, the Gomers. But beyond its impressive history, Linneman's has a

Café Carpe in Fort Atkinson, Wisconsin.

notable legacy of nurturing songwriting talent — something that's atypical in the Midwest. Being so remote from recording industry centers means that not a lot of venues in these parts worry about developing songwriter talent.

Linneman, a serious Dylan freak, is different. His weekly acoustic open mic has nurtured the intensely imagistic songs of folk-rocker Christopher Porterfield of Field Report. Linneman also watched a young man named Chris Vos grow at the acoustic open mic, and now Vos and his trio the Record Company, formed in Los Angeles in 2011, are a hot touring act at large concert venues. Their infectious blues boogie vamp "(Gotta Pick Myself Up) Off the Ground," from their first full-length album, *Give It Back to You*, reached No. 1 on *Billboard's* Adult Alternative radio play chart in spring 2016, and the grunge-blues power trio has played on TV's *Conan* and *The Late Show with Stephen Colbert*.

Vos says his success goes straight back to the precociousness that tavern-owner Linneman saw in him. "The open-mic nights [at Linneman's] were instrumental in my development," he says. "It gives you [the] chance to grow. It's about creation and experimentation.

That's a wonderful thing for a young artist. Jim cares very deeply about the art, and protects it. He lets people express themselves with a chance to be heard."

Vos, incidentally, grew up on his family's dairy farm just outside of Burlington, Wisconsin. "On the farm," he says, "you wake up in the morning and you work, and when you're done you find more work to do. You don't sit around and watch TV. That kind of work ethic helps when you're in a band, because you have to do a lot of different jobs."

Across the Milwaukee River from Linneman's is Shank Hall, perhaps the most wide-ranging small venue in the region, with a broad array of indie and progressive rock, classic jazz, and other genres regularly on the lineup.

Shank is nondescript from the front, except for the overhanging theater-style back-lit marquee. Inside is a stage big enough to hold last fall's Amy Winehouse tribute show with a 15-piece orchestra. The walls hold scads of autographed black-and-white promo photos of rock and roots stars who've played here. In the very back, far from the stage and seats, is the bar, but waiters never solicit drinks during the

music.

Shank can feel like a juke joint, a honky-tonk, or a South Side Chicago blues club depending on what's going on inside. But no matter what style's on tap, it's always about the music.

From Milwaukee, head west on I-94 to Highway 26 and then turn south to arrive at Fort Atkinson's Café Carpe. Carpe co-owner Bill Camplin is also a singer-songwriter and a dedicated Dylanologist who knows the importance of setting and presentation when it comes to live music. He's created a listening room atmosphere where an audience can home in on each expressive nuance of a performance.

The room's listening space has about 70 seats and is fully separated from the café's diner and bar. An enclosed breezeway balcony beyond the performance space overlooks a rain garden and the shore of the Rock River. Carpe is well known among locals as the formative home of Janesville native Jeffrey Foucault. He and his singer-songwriter wife, Kris Delmhorst, and their sometime-bandmate Milwaukee-based Peter Mulvey, often return to perform. Like Linneman's in Milwaukee, Carpe has helped develop a number of young talents, but Camplin, a singer-

"More people are finding that a house concert is the way to go. A reason to see the show is that there's more interaction. It's more personal [than a club show], and that makes a difference."

Kiki Schueler

songwriter himself, tries to raise the bar for them, as an exacting booker and light-touch mentor. He strives to help young performers shed their self-seriousness while remaining expressive and informal. He doesn't really coach young artists but will happily sit in with them and instruct by example.

Since opening in 1985, Carpe been a constant troubadour's beacon in the northerly trail from Chicago to Milwaukee, Madison, and the Twin Cities. Camplin's partner, Kitty Welch, runs much of the operation, and their son, singer-songwriter/producer Satchel Paige Welch, deftly handles the sound when he's not working on a record in Nashville.

No Place Like Home

In Madison, the High Noon Saloon and the Crystal Corner Bar are your typical live music clubs with their own distinctive charms, but it's Kiki's House of Righteous Music that stands out in this college town.

Kiki Schueler's house, a modest ranch house on Madison's northeast side, can be spotted by the large, primitive wood sculpture of an acoustic guitar on Schueler's front lawn. There's a sunny room upstairs and in the back that she's appropriated as a green room for her artists. Schueler's basement pulls the audience close on its 40 seats for an intimate performance, facilitating easy audience-performer interaction. The walls hold dozens of colorful concert posters from venues far beyond Wisconsin. It feels like a superfan's fever dream, which is what it is for the hostess.

"It's a win-win for audience and performer and me," she says, her eyes glowing under strung Christmas lights. "But all the money goes to [the] band and staging. I make no money. More people are finding that a house concert is the way to go. A reason to see the show

is that there's more interaction. It's more personal [than a club show], and that makes a difference. What's also important to me is that a good story gets told. It's easy to relate to singer-songwriters who tell a story."

Missouri band the Bottle Rockets have played at Schueler's house six times. "It's really hard to book club dates," says the band's lead singer and songwriter Brian Henneman. "But with a house concert, it sure is easy to load in and out. And we can put out an APB on our website [saying,] 'We're looking for house concerts in this city, this city, and this city.'"

On the opposite end of the venue spectrum from Kiki's basement is the Stoughton Opera House — a venue as grand as it is intimate. It is an old, Midwestern, small-town opera house that's been refurbished with a powerful musical vision and execution. The opera house, with its imposing bell tower, is 20 miles southeast of Madison on Highway 51. It's been going for 15 increasingly successful seasons, thanks to remarkable acoustics and a sparkling annual lineup of more than 60 concerts a year, almost all devoted to roots music.

"It's one of the best-sounding rooms in the country," gushes Foucault. "The room was designed so that an unamplified voice could be heard from every seat. A band plays loudly at their own peril. I walk out to the lip of the stage in the middle of a full band set and sing through the air, and it reminds everyone that that's the way that music was heard for most of human history, until fairly recently. It feels right."

Foucault goes on to comment on what the Opera House and the city of Stoughton have accomplished together, contrasting it with gentrification in many American cities (which he calls "money chasing itself around"). Often, cities upgrade without average folks or small businesspeople being able to get by, much less get ahead. But in

Stoughton, he says, "they subsidize music and art — cultural capital — a couple nights a week, all through the year, and look what it does for the town, for the local hotels and businesses, the bars and restaurants, and ultimately the whole region. They bring in top-notch performers, treat them well and kindly, and pay them fairly, and they take production value seriously. The results speak for themselves."

The Stoughton Opera House has

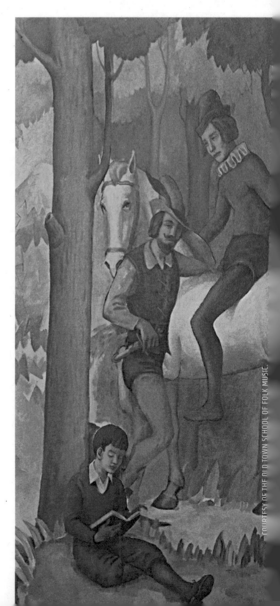

improbably grown to such ambitious success since renovating a 1901 building that by the 2007 reclamation had a hole in the roof through which you could look up and see the sky. That fact reminds me of Three Brothers Farm: how a roots music community grows through cycles of sun and moonlight, as well as deftly cultivated land and place.

In fact, the success of places as variant as Three Brothers and Stoughton Opera House raises the question: Why and how does roots music resonate so fully in the Upper Midwest?

"I think it goes back to a multi-generational experience and a sense of family," muses Stoughton Opera House director Bill Brehm. "These kinds of musical genres, and almost all musical sound, are passed from one generation of players to the next, and from one listener to the next. Each generation has something to contribute. ... The feeling of family or connectedness through different generations gives people an assurance about the continuity of life."

Perhaps this dogged effort toward functional and cultural harmony in a frequently divided world is what the roots music community, at its best, is about. And maybe it's no surprise that such harmony — like so many independent-minded roots musicians — has found a cozy home in the heart-land. ■

Mural celebrating music and nature at the Old Town School of Folk Music in Chicago.

The Faint

HEARTLAND OF DARKNESS

Examining the outgrowths of "heartland rock"

by Katherine Turman

MUSIC OFTEN HAS A strong sense of place. New Orleans, for example, gave us jazz. Oklahoma churned out the Tulsa Sound of the '50s and '60s. Los Angeles produced hair metal in the 1980s, and Seattle gave us grunge a decade later. These and other organic scenes evolved from a confluence of locale and people — shared geography, influences, and concerns expressed through song. Or at least that was the case before the internet turned the local global, making even the tiniest burgeoning regional scenes discoverable via social media.

From the late 1970s through the early '80s, the American Midwest, generally accepted to be a dozen states in the north central United States, became the de facto home to "heartland rock." The radio-friendly genre arose from agrarian roots, a definite country/ Americana brand of heartfelt, plainspoken, guitar-driven rock. And, if heartland rock is understood to be both *of* and *from* the heartland, John Mellencamp is one of its leading artists.

In "Rain on the Scarecrow," the Indiana-born singer-songwriter lays bare the region's troubles and scenes:

Rain on the scarecrow,
blood on the plow
The crops we grew last summer
weren't enough to pay the loans ...
This land fed a nation,
this land made me proud
And son I'm just sorry
there's no legacy for you now.

Other heartland rockers, meanwhile, comment on the Midwest by contrasting it with the temptations of the coasts. When Michigan-born Bob Seger's "Hollywood Nights" hero heads west, he's overwhelmed by a gorgeous California girl:

He was a Midwestern boy on his own
She looked at him with those soft eyes
So innocent and blue
He knew right then
he was too far from home.

Leavenworth, Kansas-born Melissa Etheridge shares a similar sentiment in the song "California," where she sings about leaving her roots to realize her hopes:

I took my family's burden
and I strapped it to my chest
With 100 bucks and a kiss for luck,
I pointed my dreams west
To California
Come rescue me.

"I think the press and others put the title of 'heartland rock' on music that [has], at its very core, a rock and roll and country flair," says Etheridge. "It's got that feeling of that original acoustic, story-driven music that came from the Appalachian Mountains and came down to mix with rock and roll in Memphis, and then moved up into artists such as Bob Seger and John Mellencamp and Bruce Springsteen." And while heartland rock still reigns on classic rock radio, newer bands

emerging from the Midwest aren't necessarily exploring or appropriating the musicality or lyrical issues of their heartland forebears.

Home Away from Home

For The Faint — a band that came up in the Midwest 20 years after Mellencamp and 30 after Seger — the world is bigger than their Omaha, Nebraska, hometown and experiences. "New bands are not from where they are from," says The Faint frontman Todd Fink. "They are all from the internet now. The music we were exposed to as teenagers made more of a fingerprint on the art we make than which state we happened to have picked up a guitar in."

Indeed, with albums like 2001's new-wavey *Danse Macabre,* "The Faint doesn't sound like they're from earth, let alone the Midwest," says *Omaha World-Herald* music critic Kevin Coffey.

The Faint member Dapose is likewise not of a place or time: His Vverevvolf Grehv side project is a mishmash of death and speed metal, the ideas of atheist author Howard Bloom (*The God Problem: How a Godless Cosmos Creates*), Japanese noise pioneer Merzbow, and IDM (intelligent dance music).

The Faint's hometown of Omaha — with an estimated population of 443,885 in the city proper — has a rich and diverse musical history, from influential black musicians in the 1920s all the way to the indie-rock "Omaha Sound" spawned and nurtured by the label Saddle Creek records starting in the mid-'90s.

Hear Nebraska managing editor Andrew Stellmon says that there "isn't really a culturally ingrained style of music throughout the state. Omaha maintains a strong indie, garage, and DIY rock scene; Lincoln has a robust folk and roots community. There are pockets of soul and funk and a big jam band/EDM following, even if it's kinda under the radar. There's even a swath of up-and-coming rappers — a few of them really talented and forward-thinking."

Yet the state maintains a kind of rootsy allure for music fans from elsewhere, who perceive it as a sort of middle-of-nowhere. Perhaps this is due to the fact that it was called out by Jersey boy Bruce Springsteen in his dark, stark 1982 album *Nebraska*, via the title track about Charles Starkweather. With his teenage girlfriend Caril Ann Fugate, Starkweather murdered 11 people over an eight-day period in 1958. The song has been covered by several other artists, including the Midwest-sounding Steve Earle and actual Midwesterner Chrissie Hynde, an Ohioan who fled to England to find her true musical home — and bandmates — in the Pretenders.

As is true of many Midwesterners who wander away from the region's folksy image without abandoning its influence, with a Brit band behind her, Hynde's lyrics often reflected the environmental and social concerns of her upbringing. "My City was Gone," for example, described the development that destroyed the "pretty countryside" of her Akron, Ohio, childhood, which was "paved down the middle by a government that had no pride / The

farms of Ohio had been replaced by shopping malls."

The Music as a Movement

With the rise of heartland rock, the term "heartland" developed a rootsy musical pastiche in the early 1980s. As *The New York Times* critic Jon Pareles wrote in 1987, "Mr. [Bruce] Springsteen got the heartland-rock bandwagon rolling with *The River* in 1980 and its bleak 1982 successor, *Nebraska*." With *Born in the USA* (1984), he noted, heartland rock became a "full-fledged movement, one that Mr. Mellencamp joined in 1985 with *Scarecrow*."

Of course, there's some irony in calling coastal artists "heartland rockers." Springsteen is a New Jersey native who manages to strike a working-class chord not only on the coasts, but in the smallest corners of Middle America. Ditto Florida's Tom Petty, who's written his share of poignant songs about the "American Girl." Conversely, there are actual heartlanders, like middle-of-the-road Champaign, Illinois, rock group REO Speedwagon, who have never been fully embraced as heartland rock, though they wrote lyrics like, "A woman can't be high-class in a lonely farmer's town / And the son of a poor man ain't gonna turn your head around."

San Antonio, Texas, native Steve Earle is often pigeonholed into the heartland category, even though he moved to Nashville at the age of 19 and is now, at 61, a New Yorker who travels to Texas to record. Earle acknowledges that his music — packed with working-class heroes and the kind of everyday, salt-of-the-earth themes that no doubt appeal to his Midwestern audience — has been a product of his environment. (If he'd been born in, say, France, he asserts, he has "no doubt" that he'd be a completely different musician.)

"I want to think of myself as having this vast blue-collar audience in the heartland, [but] the truth of the matter is I've kinda been an NPR act," Earle says. Nonetheless, he adds that "*Guitar Town* [his 1986 debut album] got written because I saw the *Born in the USA* tour [1984-85]. I've seen Springsteen a lot, but for some reason that clicked that I needed to go home and write a record. I wrote *Guitar Town*, and everything changed for me."

While many critics don't seem to have a problem employing "heartland rock" to describe music by artists like Earle who have never lived in the heartland, there are a fair share of lifelong heartlanders who don't identify with the form. *Omaha World-Herald's* Coffey says that in his experience, "a lot of musicians from the Midwest are people who, especially prior to the internet, were looking for something, anything, different from what they were finding at home.

"I really hate the characterization of the Midwest as some kind of backwater without electricity," he adds, "but unless you live in one of the larger cities, you might grow up in a small town with no record store or with only a few radio stations, so you look elsewhere. I know people who would drive to Omaha to go to the record store. Or pore over mail order catalogs for new records."

Prog in the Prairie

Though some artists have sought a sound and identity beyond their hometowns, other bands have taken their pride of place to the nth degree — in a name: Kansas, Black Oak Arkansas, Chilliwack, Chicago.

Rich Williams, guitarist and co-founder of the "heartland prog" band

Kansas, was raised in Topeka, but explains that it was the "fact" of music more than a particular style native to his area that was his major spark in the good/bad old days before internet and cable TV.

"You had these ads on the AM stations that broadcast across several states," he says. "You'd hear, 'This Friday night at the Hollyhock Ballroom in Hatfield, Minnesota, will be the Fabulous Flippers!'

"There's something magical about sitting in your bedroom, lights off, before bed, the radio on, and you're hearing these ads from this faraway land," he recalls. "It was all these big 10-piece show bands, in matching suits with a horn section, Hammond organ, and they're very soulful bands, playing the soul hits of the day, which is not what I ended up doing, obviously. But there was something that intrigued me."

Indeed, for many young, hopeful musicians, seeing and hearing touring bands who are only slightly older than they are is often more of a catalyst to create than the actual style or content of the music itself.

The coming-of-age of Fink of Omaha's The Faint bears out that hypothesis. "By the time I had learned to play a little I found myself at a local show some friends had brought me to see," he remembers. "It was a local Omaha band called Slowdown Virginia [later to become Cursive]. It triggered something in me — a vision, or an ambition or something. They reminded me how customizable, exciting, and expressive music can be. Although The Faint doesn't necessarily sound similar to Simon Joyner, Cursive, Bright Eyes, or any of the other bands who have come out of Omaha, I think that we are each expressions of the same supportive Omaha music scene."

Twenty-some years earlier, before Fink's musical awakening, Kansas' Williams had a similar epiphany. "One summer night there was a block party the next street over," he says. "I had my windows open and I could hear a band

Kansas

playing — a local version of one of these roving soul bands traveling the Midwest circuit. They were playing 'Land of 1000 Dances' [written in 1962, made famous by Wilson Pickett in 1966]. I'm lying there, and I didn't know what I was hearing but I wanted to be over there. But more than that, I wanted to know what that was, like a little boy who wanted to join the circus. At that moment, I had a taste of what I wanted to be. Not just to go to the circus, I wanted to be *in* the circus."

In a 2014 article titled "Prog Rock Was Famous in the Midwest? Or, The Land That Yes Fertilized," blogger Carwreck deBangs wonders about

London-bred prog pioneers Yes, who formed in 1968. "How did this happen that such a distinctly British and classically trained outfit would have such a huge stamp on the boogie rock denizens of the heartland of America?" deBangs writes. "Images of Midwest America in the '70s are mostly replete with pick-up trucks, farms, Daisy Dukes, open beers, and outdoor parties cranking kickass rock music. But Moog synthesizers, complex time signatures, Tolkien-esque lyrics and velvet? How the hell did this happen?"

For the members of Kansas, at least, one answer comes via violinist David Ragsdale, who joined the band in 1991.

Ragsdale believes it has a great deal to do with the individual members' youthful classical influences — his own included. The Memphis-born, Alabama- and Georgia-bred Ragsdale says, "Kansas is a marriage of rock and classical. That's kind of the definition of prog rock, but it's a real happy marriage."

Indeed, founding violinist Robby Steinhardt was classically trained from the age of eight. He was the son of the director of the music history department at the University of Kansas and, as a young violinist, played with orchestras in Europe.

"But the guys [in Kansas] also rocked, so it turned out to be a happy marriage," furthers Ragsdale. "Prog tends to be prog from start to finish. Kansas tends to rock and prog and rock and prog. When it goes into the more lyrical passages — it's very sweeping. Everyone in the band listened to classical music. They understood it and incorporated it.

"Both my parents had bachelors and masters in music," he adds. "I was dragged, kicking and screaming, to the classical [music]. It was my destiny to play the violin, but as a kid I had no interest in it. I wanted to play the guitar. I wanted to be a Beatle."

By 16, however, he adds, "My head

Steve Earle

had already been turned by Jean Luc Ponty and Jerry Goodman of the Mahavishnu Orchestra. Then I heard Kansas on the radio for the first time; this rocking band with this rockin' violin player [Steinhardt]."

Kansas, who formed in Topeka in 1973 and recently released *The Prelude Implicit*, their 15th album (and first in 16 years), is easily the best-known example of a group *from* the heartland but not *of* it. They're named after the 34th state, yet they don't appear to be influenced musically or topically by local music tradition or the concerns of their community. To wit, the 1977 Kansas single "Portrait (He Knew)" is about Albert Einstein.

> He had a thousand ideas,
> you might have heard his name
> He lived alone with his vision
> Not looking for fortune or fame ...
> He was off on another plane
> The words that he said were a mystery
> Nobody's sure he was sane.

Their music is often equally idiosyncratic — 4/4 and 3/4 time signatures, phrased as 4+4+4+3 in the verses, a 4/4 prechorus and the main chorus phrased in 7/4 time — a changeup that's a hallmark of prog rock or jazz. Kansas, then, is a band from "smack dab in the middle" (as Williams puts it) who sound like they grew up in London alongside bands like Yes, the Nice, and the Moody Blues. Co-founder and drummer Phil Ehart even went to England to look for musicians before returning to the states to form the group.

Ragsdale, who has a bachelor's degree in violin performance, believes "There is an enormous amount of Americana in Kansas music, but it's offset by the European influences that creep in and destroy everything from time to time — which is why we get to hang out with the rock dudes."

Even the band's artwork has a classical tinge. The image on their debut album hangs in the Metropolitan Museum (by John Steuart Curry of abolitionist John Brown); *Leftoverture* has a "Renaissance" feel. British-born illustrator Peter Lloyd, who would later

earn more prog credits doing digital effects for the 1982 film *Tron*, created the band's *Song for America* cover as well as the iconic *Point of Know Return* illustration of a sailing ship falling off the "end" of an ocean.

The landlocked teens — three hours from the geographical center of the country in Lebanon, Kansas — had visions beyond any borders, and with apologies to Yes and their 18-minute opus, sought to get closer to the edge, musically, visually, and lyrically.

"Lyrically, the Beach Boys have sung yearning songs forever about girls, and that's great. I love them," says Williams. "But do we need to do that too? There were other subjects to sing about." Less plainspoken ones.

And millions of Americans bought — literally — the band's progressive rock-tinged hits. Notably, 1977's quadruple-platinum *Point of Know Return* was the band's apogee. "Dust in the Wind" and the disc's title track, which clocked in at a radio-friendly 3:13, became and remain FM radio staples. Not everyone "got it," though. At the time, *Rolling Stone* called

"I really hate the characterization of the Midwest as some kind of backwater without electricity, but unless you live in one of the larger cities, you might grow up in a small town with no record store or with only a few radio stations, so you look elsewhere."

Kevin Coffey

the *Point of Know Return* album "a wan and ridiculous rehash of the bargain-basement exoticism employed by the British art-rock crowd."

Going Viral, Slowly

Starcastle is another Midwestern lineup who looked to Yes and were overtly Euro and prog rock in sound and stylings. *Fountains of Light*, the group's second album, released in 1977 and helmed by Queen producer Roy Thomas Baker, was characterized by a 10-minute-plus opening track. Ironically, Yes keyboardist Rick Wakeman's son Oliver joined Starcastle in 2007.

Kansas/Missouri-based band Shooting Star formed in the '70s, and, like Kansas, employed keys, violin, and an often-sweeping musicality. In fact, they moved to the UK for a time, and sounded so Euro that they became the first American band signed to British-bred record label Virgin, their "You've Got What I Need" breaking into the *Billboard* Hot #100.

Illinois-based Styx were another epic vocalizing, keyboard-forward Midwestern lineup. Concept albums like *Kilroy Was Here*, featuring "Mr. Roboto," is a far cry from "heartland rock," though their melding of prog influences and concepts netted several multiplatinum albums and more than a dozen Top-40 singles over decades of success.

Heartland rock had a darker tinge in Michigan. Detroit, the Midwest's fourth-largest city, is known for its transgressive rockers. While Ted Nugent and Bob Seger may be the heavier entries in the heartland rock world, oddballs are the norm from this once-booming manufacturing hub. Iggy Pop and the Stooges, the MC5, and black political proto-punk band Death all flew in the face of conformity, spewing aggro, politically charged tunes rather than sorrowful paeans to Midwestern life.

As Death co-founder Bobby Hackney remembers, "when we were making this music in 1975, the term 'punk' hadn't even been coined as a musical phrase. If you called somebody a punk in Detroit in 1975, you got one of two things: a black eye or a bloody nose. So we were just playing hard-driving Detroit rock and roll." These one-time anomalies enjoyed a rediscovery thanks to 2012's engaging documentary *A Band Called Death*.

That's not to say that distinct musical influences from thousands of miles away didn't creep into the musical culture back in the day. It just took longer. For metal kids in the early '80s, "tape trading" was the way music was spread internationally. A teenager in San Francisco would send a tape of a favorite local band to a fellow metalhead in Denmark. And like that '80s Fabergé Organics shampoo commercial said, they told two friends, "and so on, and so on, and so on." Thus, "going viral" took

months. Metallica's Lars Ulrich was one of those tape traders in the years before he formed the biggest metal band in the world. Ditto Brian Slagel, who went on to form influential label Metal Blade Records.

In 1977, a music lover in, say, Devil's Lake, North Dakota, would be hard-pressed to find a local record store that carried the Sex Pistols or a place that sold the UK's weekly musical bibles, *Melody Maker* and *NME (New Musical Express)* magazines. Pre-internet, scenes and information were largely regional unless a band broke out on the radio. To expand your musical vocabulary, you needed to be an intrepid music lover, and hard-working, too: "It was more difficult then than it is now, for sure," says Coffey. "But if you were that into music, you'd quickly outgrow the local radio station and seek musical satisfaction wherever you could."

Melissa Etheridge says her early influences "came from the radio and from the music that my family and my friends bought and partook in. The radio was very, very influential to me. First I had the AM radio, WHB in Kansas City, and I was blessed because that was music that was pop and rock and country and Motown and soul. You could hear Tammy Wynette and Led Zeppelin and Tommy James and the Shondells and Marvin Gaye all in one hour. It was this beautiful, beautiful mix of music that really became the music I was playing."

On tour, Etheridge travels across the United States, where she observes that "every city has its own music scene, whether it's very, very small or whether it's a booming one. ... Local music will always be where everything comes from; everyone needs to start somewhere." Technology, however, has made geography-tied underground scenes a thing of the past. The musicians may be local, but the music is often inter-nationally influenced. These days, a young musician growing up in the shadow of Tulsa's famed Cain's Ballroom, the home of Western swing star Bob Wills and his Texas Playboys, might be more influenced by German acid house music, despite a proximity to local musical history and legends.

It wasn't so easy to broaden your musical horizons in the early '70s, but it wasn't impossible, as Earle, growing up in the rich musical stew of Texas, recalls: "A friend who I went to high school with played me the first Elvis Costello record and all of a sudden I wanted an electric guitar for the first time. The first Elvis record was kind of a mind-blower, and coincidentally, the Sex Pistols were playing at Randy's Rodeo in San Antonio [now Randy's Ballroom, a Tejano club], like four blocks from where I grew up. I saw them there. Shitty gig. Sid got hit in the head with a beer bottle and bled

through the gig and there was no bass."

Farm Aid Sows Fans

Earle may embody or admire some of the Pistols' bad-boy attitude, but his image is more along the lines of do-gooding and activism. For starters, he's played at Farm Aid seven times. The annual benefit concert, launched in 1985 in Champaign, Illinois, and spearheaded by Mellencamp, Neil Young, and Willie Nelson, ties heartland music to family farmers and their challenges, raising national consciousness of both. The first Farm Aid raised over $9 million for America's family farmers, and Nelson and Mellencamp were active in urging Congress to pass the Agricultural Credit Act of 1987 to help save family farms from foreclosure.

If "heartland rock" had begun to wane as a specific genre by the early 1990s, Farm Aid has continued to shine a light on heartland-influenced music, family farms, and agricultural issues, with musical draws including relatable American artists such as Stevie Ray Vaughan, Arlo Guthrie, Lynyrd Skynyrd, Kasey Musgraves, and the BoDeans at its annual shindigs.

And, as Adam Sheets opined on nodepression.com in 2010, "By 1989 the genre was fading from the mainstream, and the last relatively well-known artist to debut in the genre may have been

James McMurtry, with his John Mellencamp-produced debut *Too Long in the Wasteland*. ... This is where the alt-country/Americana and heartland rock roads, both of which arguably began with John Fogerty, meet. Many fans and artists of the [heartland] genre went on to discover that performers like Steve Earle, Uncle Tupelo, and the Bottle Rockets [weren't] really all that different than the music we loved."

Indeed, music genres morph and wax and wane, though many of the original wave of heartland bands are still making music and topping charts — including Mellencamp and Kansas, who are on the road with new music, new members, and a slate of dramatic hits.

Hear Nebraska's Stellmon believes that heartland rock "kind of happened as a phenomenon and then disappeared once the style fell out of favor. I suppose Springsteen is forever tied to the genre, regardless of location," he says, calling the Boss "arguably on the Mount Rushmore of heartland rock."

Ultimately, he adds, "There just aren't many artists playing that style of music around here. If 'heartland rock' has to exist, I'd define it much differently than the Seger/Mellencamp/Springsteen crowd. That genre either exists in a small way or is really different from what it used to be. If we redefined it from scratch today, it wouldn't be the same." ■

"Every city has its own music scene, whether it's very, very small or whether it's a booming one. ... Local music will always be where everything comes from; everyone needs to start somewhere."

Melissa Etheridge

BEAN BLOSSOM BRIDGE
1880

Reverend Peyton (right) with
His Big Damn Band.

Keep Manhattan, Just Give Me That Countryside

by Reverend Peyton

T EN YEARS AGO, A MUSIC industry friend informed me "You need to move to East Nashville or Austin."

"Why?" I asked. "My home is here in Indiana."

"Because things are happening there," my friend said. "Industry people are there, and people will take you more seriously if you are in one of those places."

I've heard a similar tune from a number of different folks over the years. Sometimes they tell me I have to move to Portland, sometimes it's L.A., sometimes it's Brooklyn. I didn't believe it the first time I heard this from a music industry friend, and I don't believe it now.

Call it stubborn, but I need to be true to myself, too. Maybe I have the same Southern Indiana stubbornness that inspired John Mellencamp to stay here and write songs like "Small Town" and "Scarecrow." Maybe I just didn't want to be another mouse in the city, chasing a tiny piece of cheese. There's probably some great truth in both of those things,

but deep down I always felt like I didn't need to move to any of those places; I just needed to take myself and my music to those places ... and then come home.

In 2005, my Big Damn Band and I were invited to perform at the Midwest Music Summit in Indianapolis. I went to one panel while we were there. The names of the speakers on the panel escape me, but there were people with *No Depression*, Ear X-tacy in Louisville (which doesn't exist anymore), and others. One of the panel speakers asked the crowd, "When was the last time you bought a CD because of an advertisement?"

"I don't think ever," someone in the audience responded.

"Never," they responded, "and your whole life is music." Making a point about the value of advertising for independent artists, the panelist then said, "Save your money, buy a van, and tour."

That settled it. In June 2006, we sold everything we owned, moved into a van, and set out on the road full-time.

The first year was tough. We barely made enough money to buy food and gasoline. The strings on my guitars were almost always weeks or months old. Thanks to a steady diet of ramen noodles and whatever was free or given to us, our health suffered. The shows were far apart and routed like someone threw darts at a map. We had to take what we could get. Yet it didn't take long before something started to happen.

Without the "music industry" noticing, fans started coming out to our shows. They started telling their friends about a front porch blues band that didn't come out of a hipster neighborhood in a big music town. Thanks to the internet and word of mouth, where we lived didn't matter. The next year, my wife and I bought a house back in Indiana. Those Southern Indiana hills called to me. My rural upbringing inspired all of my songs — how could I abandon that? If I had moved to a big city and worked a service job while trying to be discovered, I think I wouldn't have a music career at all. My music is too unique, too outside of normal formats, and the old model is dead. Besides, we've heard that story before.

I wanted to tell the story of all the country-ass people I grew up with. These folks are just trying to carve out a life with what they know and what they have. They are good people with faults and foibles, but they are good people. Besides, when you grow up in a rural area, the lack of hustle and bustle allows you to spend more time with your instrument.

I grew up around some astounding pickers. The coasts and the big cities sometimes forget that people like us exist. My family consists of construction workers, farmers, mechanics, service workers, and such. These are people who work with their hands, and I have to wonder who would tell their stories if I moved to a hipster neighborhood in a big city and tried to pretend I was from a cooler-sounding place than Indiana?

What is "cool" anymore, anyway? I stopped caring what the music industry thought was cool long ago. Do you think record executives or anyone could tell Muddy Waters what was cool? No! Muddy Waters told *them* what was cool. The same can be said for Johnny Cash, Hank Sr., Chuck Berry, Charley Patton, or anyone in American music history who had a real voice that mattered.

My band has played handmade music in 48 of the 50 states, in 32 other countries, on four continents. I love visiting all those places, but I wouldn't want to ever leave my home in the hills of Brown County, Indiana. Indiana may not be a perfect place — there are invariably ways all people and places can improve — but it's home to me.

In case you were thinking of moving here, there are snakes and bugs and coyotes and dirt. You city folks wouldn't like it. ∎

SOUND VIBRATIONS

How a small label in Indiana changed the world

by Stephen Deusner

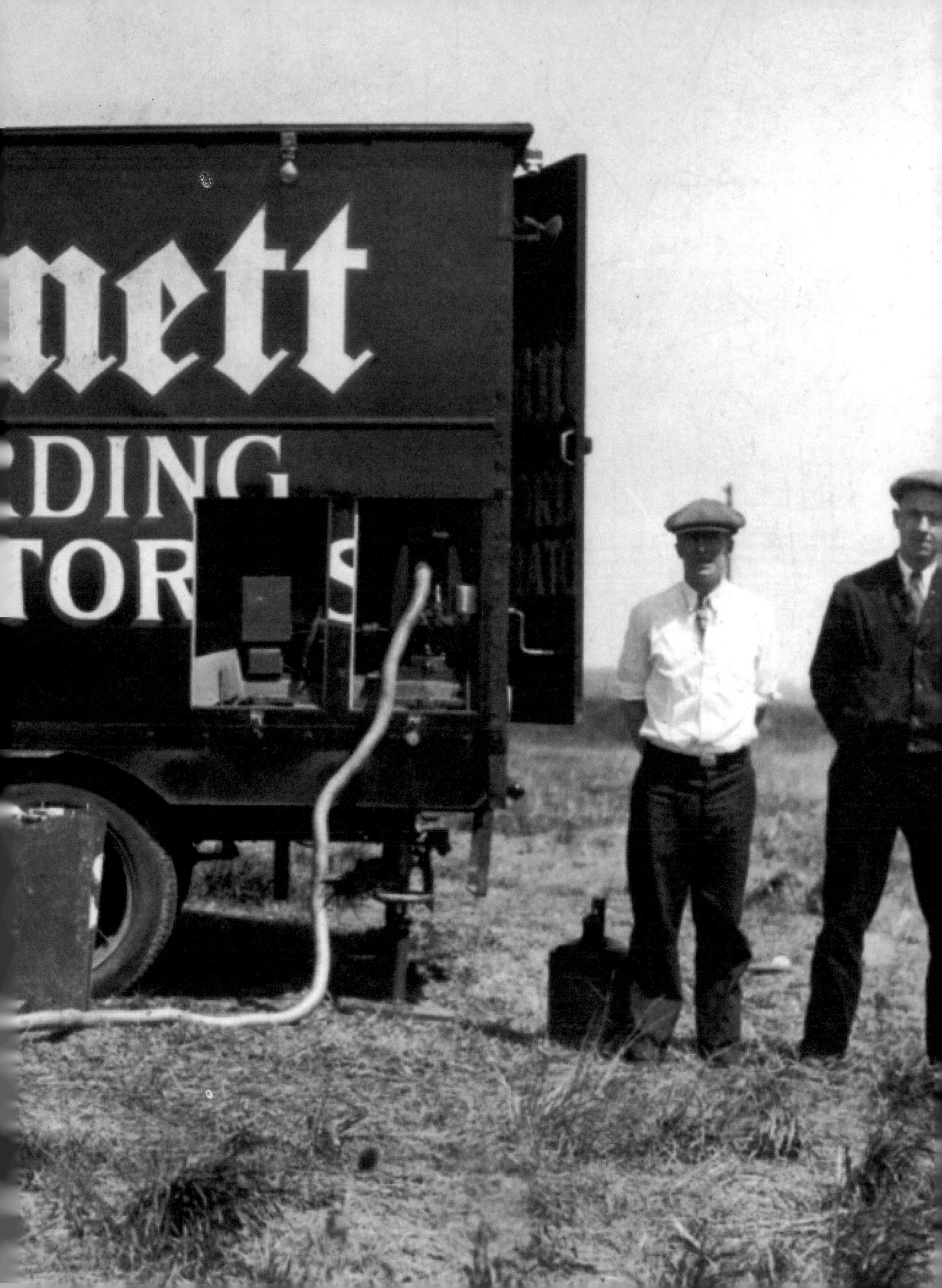
nett
RDING
TOR S

CHARLEY PATTON STARES out from the green-blue brick wall in Richmond, Indiana, with unblinking eyes. He's seated in a chair, legs crossed to show off his spats, a bowtie at his neck, his suit a few sizes too big. His hair is mottled against the brick, his nose bulges, his ears sit mismatched on either side of a head too small for its body. Those eyes are slightly askew, lending him a quizzical countenance, as though he has just posed a question and doesn't understand your response. Across his lap, he holds a Stella acoustic guitar, proud and cocky, his left hand draped over the top of the neck and his fingers spidering onto the frets. The paint on his fingers has been applied awkwardly, inexactly, but the impression might be purposeful: More than 80 years after his death, Charley Patton doesn't want to reveal too much about his technique.

Based on the only known photo of the Mississippi bluesman, this black-and-white mural was painted by Charles Guess as part of the 2011 Festival of Murals in Richmond. For five years, Patton has been staring out from the building on 9th and Main, which stands vacant today, a two-dimensional stalactite streak of rust from the adjacent fire escape cutting into his shoulder. Above him, written in an ornate script, is the name Charlie Patton — the alternative spelling. It's impossible to imagine what those inscrutable eyes have seen in five years. How many times do the locals pass him by each day? Enough that they no longer notice him? Or enough that he has become a local himself?

Patton was the first of the great Delta bluesmen, exerting an incalculable influence on popular American music throughout the 20th century and well into the 21st, and this isn't the only public image of him in Richmond. Across town, he occupies a wall alongside Eric Clapton, the Brit who learned a thing or two from the Mississippi native. At Firehouse Barbecue & Blues, a framed photo of the bluesman watches patrons chow down on pulled pork sandwiches and Ball jars of baked beans. Down in Whitewater River Gorge Park is a large plaque in the shape of a record, bearing Patton's likeness in an elaborate mosaic. Despite years of exposure to weather and foot traffic, its pieces retain their bold colors. This medallion, one of many in Richmond celebrating various blues, jazz, and county musicians, has the look of stained glass, of something holy.

How did so many images of Charley Patton end up in a small Hoosier city 700 miles north of his home in Dockery, Mississippi? How did one of the most legendary bluesmen become a local in Richmond? And why is he not alone? You can walk all over the city, especially around Main Street and the historic Depot District, and see some of the most famous musicians of the early 20th century, men and women whose work formed the bedrock of popular American music: Louis Armstrong, Hoagy Carmichael, Alberta Hunter, Gene Autry, Bix Beiderbecke, Jelly Roll Morton, Duke Ellington, Coleman Hawkins, Lonnie Johnson, Blind Lemon Jefferson, Uncle Dave Mason, Georgia Tom (aka gospel legend Thomas A. Dorsey), and many, many, many others.

The answer to all these questions is Gennett Records.

During the late 1920s, the label made the first recordings by some of the most important musicians in America, releasing tens of thousands of sides in every style and genre imaginable. Working out of a modest storeroom at the Starr Piano factory, the label established Richmond as the capital of recorded pop music in America. In fact, the history of Gennett is bound up in the history of Richmond, as important a site for musical history as New York or Chicago. And yet it remains obscure, a destination for collectors all over the world but largely unknown in most of America.

"This story needs to be front and center in the history of the recording industry," says Charlie B. Dahan, a professor of recording industry at Middle Tennessee State University who has been working for ten years to compile a complete Gennett discography. He recently co-authored a photographic history of the label called *Images of America: Gennett Records and Starr Piano* (Arcadia Publishing). "The creed of independent labels is something like, 'We can't compete with the majors so we have to do something different. We can't deal with the center, so we have to deal with what's outside. We have to bring what's outside to the inside.' That's the dynamic through the history of the industry, and that dynamic begins with Gennett."

A Culture of Music

"Richmond, Indiana, was a regional magnet for musicians to come and record," explains Bob Jacobsen. "The music they made here — blues and jazz and hillbilly records — was really a regional music until people started selling it and radio stations started playing it. People all over the country loved it, and it took off."

Few people know as much about Richmond as Jacobsen and Don Clark, two affable men past retirement age who spend much of their time down in the Starr-Gennett Foundation offices on 7th Street — about a block away from the Patton mural. The organization's goal is to preserve and promote local music history, and the pair have worked together for ten years in a variety of roles but with an escalating obsession with all things Gennett.

Located in the basement of what was once a bank, their office is busy with memorabilia: books piled high on desks, flyers and brochures arranged in tidy stacks, colorful posters advertising local jazz festivals from years past. Hanging on the wall is a map of the United States that traces the music's migration out of New Orleans and up to Richmond and Chicago, west to California, east to New York, across the Atlantic to Europe. One corner of the room is dominated by two bulky and ornate phonograph cabinets made here in Richmond nearly a century ago, a testament to its once flourishing furniture industry. It's a lively office, so much colorful musical ephemera eradicating the institutional ambience of cinderblock walls and drop-tile ceiling.

Richmond's rich musical history is, Clark and Jacobsen explain, dependent on its unique geography. "There is more fall in elevation from the north end of the county to the sound end of the county than there is from the Canadian border to the Gulf of Mexico," says Clark, the older of the two. The highest spot in the state — Hoosier Hill, 1,257 ft. — is located in the northwest corner of Wayne County, and it's all downhill from there. This dramatically sloping terrain creates a strong, steady current that courses through regional waterways, including the Whitewater River that runs through Richmond. Too shallow for transportation, that river provided power to local tanneries and gristmills, turning Richmond into a Midwestern hub for water power industries.

Those factors made Richmond incredibly prosperous, creating a culture of industrial innovation that persisted deep into the 20th century. At one point the city was known as the Lawn Mower Capital of the World, thanks to the Dille-McGuire Company,

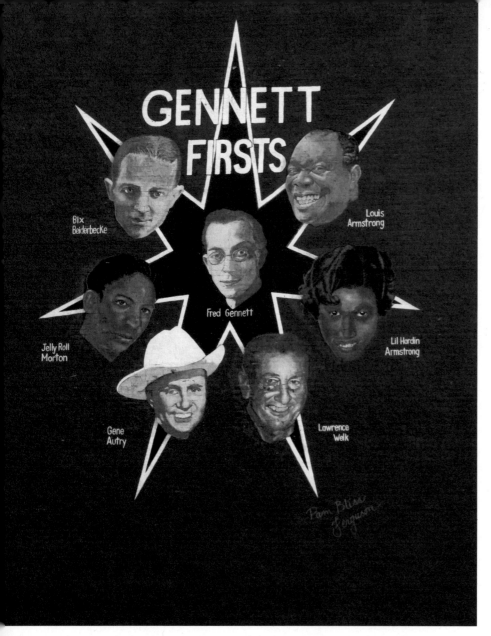

GENNETT FIRSTS

Bix Beiderbecke

Louis Armstrong

Fred Gennett

Jelly Roll Morton

Lil Hardin Armstrong

Gene Autry

Lawrence Welk

Pam Bliss Ferguson

which manufactured the machines locally into the 1960s. The Crosley Corporation built cars in Richmond and later refrigerators — including the Shelvador, the first model with shelves. The world's first car phone was developed here in 1948 by a local named Ramsey McDonald, but the Dial Direct proved too bulky and expensive to mass-produce. (Visit the Wayne County Historical Museum to see a fascinating replica.)

But the biggest industry in Richmond may have been music — in particular, pianos. "Back in the 1800s," says Jacobsen, "the piano was something a lot of families wanted in their parlor. You wanted your children to learn how to play it. That was an evening's entertainment."

"The piano was an early home entertainment center," Clark adds with a chuckle.

In the late 19th and early 20th century, before the advent of recording technology, music was disseminated via sheet music, which notated both classical and popular songs and made celebrities of such composers as Irving Berlin and John Philip Sousa. But sheet music won't play itself. Consumers needed something to play it on, spurring a corresponding boom in piano manufacturing, especially in Richmond. At its 35-acre factory in the Whitewater Gorge, a glacial indention along the Whitewater River, the Starr Piano Company employed around 700 locals to produce instruments of various size, sound, and expense — from miniature pianolas to massive uprights. The company needed skilled workers to

build these elaborate instruments and carve the wood, so Starr recruited craftsmen from Germany, paying to bring their families across the Atlantic to Indiana. "Starr brought in so many German families that it had quite an effect on the city's culture," says Clark. "In fact, I was told by one member of St. John's Lutheran that there was a requirement for the pastor to speak German — all the way up into the 1940s!"

But technology does not slow down for long. In the early 1900s, piano sales were dented by the introduction of records and radio, which made music even more accessible to consumers. In 1915, the Starr Piano board of directors voted to expand the company's charter to include "the production, preservation, use and control of sound vibrations for musical, commercial, and other economic purposes." In other words, they decided to start making phonograph consoles, advertising in national magazines and selling them in their piano showrooms. Early models weren't simply turntables, but entire cabinets. This was furniture, the mechanics of the machine hidden behind elaborately designed, beautifully carved woodwork.

Just like sheet music demands a piano, phonographs need records. In 1917 Starr Piano launched Gennett Records, named for Henry Gennett, who had served as the company's secretary-treasurer and had spearheaded its expansion into "sound vibrations." For the first few years the company made all of its recordings — mostly featuring vaudeville acts — at a studio in New York City, but eventually Gennett built a studio in Richmond, making its first recordings there in 1921. The setup was primitive by today's standards, but it would have been state-of-the-art just after World War I. The rectangular building had one room, bisected by a thick curtain from which protruded an enormous horn. Musicians would play and sing into that horn, which was connected to a pedal-pump turntable on the other side of the curtain. The vibrations of the music moved a stylus that left an impression in a wax disc, which became the master from which Gennett's 78s would be pressed.

It was a precarious method at best. The stylus was so sensitive that even the slightest noises and vibrations would disrupt the recording. Drums weren't allowed in the studio, because even gentle timekeeping could throw the stylus out of its groove. Most drummers kept the beat on sticks. Even more

disruptive were the trains that frequently passed by on the trestle on the adjacent hillside, or the switchback that ran just outside the studio doors.

The larger record labels in Chicago and New York had already established a foothold in the industry, signing classical musicians and opera singers to exclusive contracts. Like other independent labels that were popping up around the same time — Paramount Records in Wisconsin, along with Vocalion, Okeh, and Columbia in the Big Apple — Gennett didn't have the money to compete for those entertainers, so the

company looked elsewhere for talent. That's where Gennett Records made its most important contribution to popular music: Priced out of highbrow artists, the label instead looked to jazz bands playing small clubs in Chicago, acts like the New Orleans Rhythm Kings and King Oliver's Creole Jazz Band. (Most of the musicians were from Louisiana but had moved north for bigger shows and greater notoriety.)

Even before rock and roll, jazz was youth music. Most of the combos were young, some barely out of their teens, and the audiences were even younger.

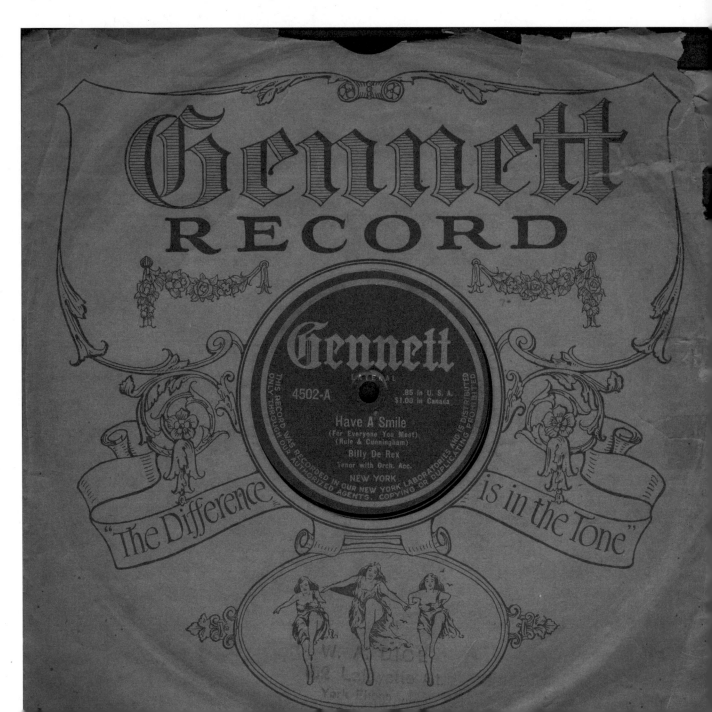

Wolverine Orchestra with Bix Beiderbecke, second from right.

Horse-drawn crates with Starr pianos.

OUR FACTORY

King Oliver's Creole Jazz Band.

"We had a lot of teenagers who recorded at Gennett," says Jacobsen. "Some of them were only 17 or 18 years old. This was the music kids wanted to listen to, so it was the music kids were playing."

"When these first records were cut, these people weren't famous," Clark adds. "They were just struggling. It's who they became a generation later or a few decades later that we recognize. Wow, how did Beiderbecke get started? What did Armstrong sound like when he was just coming out of New Orleans? Well, we have a copy of that. This is roots music for popular song."

Landmark Sessions

Jazz put Gennett Records — and, consequently, Richmond — on the map. Over the next few years the studio hosted sessions featuring some of the biggest names in popular music. Duke Ellington recorded there, as did Coleman Hawkins and Sidney Bechet. Bix Beiderbecke made some of his earliest 78s at Gennett, and Hoagy

Carmichael, then a law student at Indiana University in Bloomington, made his first recording of "Stardust" in 1927. Perhaps the most famous jazz musician to cut a record at Gennett was a young New Orleans native named Louis Armstrong, who at the time was playing in King Oliver's Creole Jazz Band. Oliver himself is a looming figure in jazz history, but his second cornetist overshadowed him.

Those sessions, held in 1923, are shrouded in legend, and one anecdote persists, perhaps apocryphal but still revealing. In that early studio, the musicians would be arranged around the room based on the volume of their instruments. Banjos and guitars were clustered near the recording horn, with trombones behind them, and trumpets and cornets a little farther back. When Armstrong soloed, however, he played so loud that he bounced the stylus off the disc. With each take he had to move farther and farther back, until he was right at the door, nearly outside of the studio.

It might be a tall tale, but it shows just how large Armstrong looms in the popular imagination.

Nearly one hundred years later, it's impossible to overestimate the importance of these sessions, which not only document the first efforts by true innovators, but introduced vernacular music as a profitable enterprise for the recording industry. Today, these 78s — which for decades were rarities but today have all been digitized to stream and download — provide a map of early American popular music. Jazz was not Gennett's only specialty, however; the label recorded gospel, hillbilly, big bands, small bands, bluegrass, novelty hits, speeches, and sound effects. In 1923 William Jennings Bryan traveled to Richmond to record his famous "Cross of Gold" speech, which he originally delivered at the 1896 Democratic National Convention. It became one of Gennett's all-time biggest sellers.

Gennett's motivation wasn't musical curiosity or some desire to document the vernacular sounds of the era.

The rectangular building had one room, bisected by a thick curtain from which protruded an enormous horn. Musicians would play and sing into that horn, which was connected to a pedal-pump turntable on the other side of the curtain. The vibrations of the music moved a stylus that left an impression in a wax disc, which became the master from which Gennett's 78s would be pressed.

Instead, it was motivated by money, which meant the label sought recordings that would not only sell themselves but would sell the phonograph cabinets. A handful of 78s might be given away free with the purchase of a Starr cabinet, or might be advertised alongside the players in magazines like *The Saturday Evening Post* and *Life*. Gennett also rented its studio to competing labels, which often licensed Gennett masters or sent their artists to Richmond for recording sessions, and to outside groups that paid to cut and press records. One of those groups was the Klu Klux Klan, which rented the studio to cut ugly inversions of popular songs and hymns for its membership.

The KKK has always had a stronghold in the Hoosier State. In fact, the day of Armstrong's legendary sessions coincided with a massive Klan rally in Richmond. On the whole, however, the racism that might have run rampant in other parts of the state didn't infiltrate the city as deeply as it did other cities, thanks to the presence of a Quaker population that was slightly more accepting of the black musicians who came to town. Even if there are no indications that whites and blacks recorded together, it is remarkable that Gennett recorded both black and white musicians at all. While the market may have segregated pop music into strict categories, the entrepreneurial impulse blurred those lines somewhat. Profit is profit. In 1927, Gennett sprouted

subsidiary imprints Electrobeam and Black Patti to sell race and gospel records. On these, as on other Gennett 78s, the scarcity of promotional photographs and the relative anonymity of the young musicians allowed a certain blurring of color, with white recordings sold as race records and black recordings occasionally marketed to white audiences.

Up from the Delta

Gennett's legacy has gradually been eclipsed by its peers, including Paramount and Okeh. MTSU's Charlie Dahan traces the label's relative obscurity to its close identification with jazz. "What's popular right now in the media is blues. Paramount had all the country blues artists, like Charley Patton and Blind Blake. The canon of blues music is centered around Paramount. That's kind of the sexy part. Gennett is primarily known for jazz, and Americans don't really relate to jazz anymore. Louis Armstrong as a cultural figure isn't as important right now as Patton or Blind Lemon Jefferson."

But the public impression of Gennett as a predominantly jazz label, if a public impression exists at all, is not entirely correct. Its roster was incredibly diverse to begin with, even more so when you factor in who recorded at Gennett for other labels. While its impact on jazz is undeniable, Gennett might also be considered a formidable blues powerhouse. Blind Lemon Jefferson

made his final recordings in Richmond, just months before he died. Blues pianist Roosevelt Sykes recorded at Gennett, as did Scrapper Blackwell and Big Bill Broonzy. Lonnie Johnson recorded on multiple sides; because he was signed to another label, he was not credited for playing guitar on several sessions or for recording unique blues-celeste tracks with Lizzie Washington.

And then there's Charley Patton.

Patton was a guitarist and entertainer living at Dockery Plantation, deep in the Mississippi Delta, renowned regionally for his lively performances and deft fretwork. Like many of his contemporaries, he sought an audience with H.C. Speir, a talent scout based in Jackson, Mississippi, who placed musicians with a number of record labels. Impressed with Patton's nimble fretwork and wide repertoire, Speir sent him to Paramount Records, who agreed to record him. However, that label happened to be constructing a new studio at the Wisconsin Chair Company's pressing plant in Grafton, Wisconsin. Which is how Patton ended up recording in Richmond.

In June 1929, Patton and Walter "Buddy Boy" Hawkins made the 750-mile journey from the Delta to Indiana. They disembarked at the busy Pacific Railroad Station, a massive brick building designed by Daniel Burnham, who was then famous for Union Station in Washington, DC, and the Flatiron Building in New York City. The two musicians walked the mile through town and found their way down into the Whitewater Gorge, where they set up in the Gennett studio. It's easy to wonder but impossible to know what they thought of that nondescript building in the middle of an industrial compound. Would they have been impressed or disappointed?

The music they recorded that day, both together and solo, betrays no shaky nerves, no crisis of confidence, and no trains rumbling through nearby. "Pony Blues" is a deft showcase for Patton's percussive guitar picking and his mercurial vocals, which sound deepest when he's reaching for the highest notes. "Screamin' & Hollerin' the Blues" is the ultimate blues lament, his voice piercing through the acetate static to deliver a harrowing cry:

> *I'm goin' away, mama,*
> *don't you wanna go?*
> *Take God to tell when*
> *I'll be back here anymore.*

His was a rougher, rawer form of the blues, much different than the urban big-band blues that had been successful throughout most of the 1920s. It set the template for the country blues that came to prominence in the 1930s and would become even more popular during the blues revival of the 1960s. Patton set the image we have of the prototypical bluesman: a black man from the Delta, picking acrobatic riffs on a weathered acoustic guitar, alone in a room, hollering a lonesome melody.

He recorded 14 sides that day in June that were released by Paramount and sold well enough for him to record 40 more before disappearing from the recording industry. He died five years later, and, despite his success, his passing was not reported in any newspaper. In fact, his grave sat unmarked for decades before John Fogerty paid for a headstone. Still, his small body of work — and especially the sides he recorded at Gennett — established him as the forerunner of Delta blues and his label as the foremost blues label in the country (although Paramount, too, would not survive the Great Depression). His songs have been covered by every generation of blues musicians, from Howlin' Wolf (who had a hit with an adaptation of "A Spoonful Blues") to Jack White (whose Third Man label has released two massive suitcase box sets of Paramount recordings) to Rev. Peyton's Big Damn Band (who recorded a full album of covers titled *Peyton on Patton* in 2011).

In his recently updated book *Jelly Roll, Bix, and Hoagy: Gennett Records and the Rise of America's Musical Grassroots* — which stands as the definitive history of the label — historian Rick Kennedy describes June 14, 1929, as "the decade's most productive single day in Mississippi Delta blues recording."

Depression and Decline

In 1925, Gennett signed a deal to sell 78s through the Sears, Roebuck and Co. catalog, which further expanded the range of music recorded in Richmond. In addition to the blues and jazz records, the label began recording more country and folk tunes — what would have been known at the time as hillbilly music. The latter half of the decade saw visits to Richmond by the radio entertainer Bradley Kincaid, the Texas singer-songwriter Vernon Dalhart, and Fiddlin' Doc Roberts. But the biggest name in Gennett's dalliance with country might be Gene Autry. Before he was known as the Singing Cowboy, the Oklahoma native was a struggling yodeler with a few records on various labels. He wrote to Gennett requesting an audition, and the label hosted sessions for him in 1930, then released 78s on its short-lived Electrobeam subsidiary. While this collaboration between artist and label didn't last long, it did produce the foundation of his recording catalog, which would be reissued to great acclaim in the 1930s.

But the Great Depression took its toll on the recording industry, gutting most independent labels and seeing others (such as Okeh and Vocalion) acquired by larger competitors. Those economic tribulations, coupled with the growing popularity of home radios, dug into record sales, and Gennett began shuttering its subsidiaries and specialty labels. In 1930 the company closed its New York studio as well as its Electrobeam imprint. By 1934, Gennett Records was gone. The studio remained and continued to cut infrequent sessions and even pressed 78s for other labels. Starr shifted all of its manufacturing to pianos and refrigerators, among other items — but not records.

One curious side project not only survived but prospered: sound effects. Harry Gennett Jr. had been recording sound effects — crickets and crowds, marching bands and falling trees, trains, planes, and automobiles — since late 1929, and sold the records to movie studios looking to update silent films for the talkie era. That business survived the Depression and flourished during the 1940s and 1950s. The company even sponsored mobile recording studios that traveled the country collecting sonic curios along the way.

By the 1960s, Starr Piano had

shuttered its Richmond facility, and much of the city's history was disregarded for decades. "In high school my last name was Gennett, but I could have been a Smith or a Jones for all anyone cared," says Linda Gennett Irmscher, who co-authored *Images of America: Gennett Records and Starr Piano* with Charlie Dahan. Her father was Harry Gennett Jr., and all she knew of the family business was sound effects. Still, she recalls, "My mother would get calls from Japan or Europe, someone wanting to know about Gennett Records. Could they come and touch the ground where those records were made? My sister and I thought it was weird."

It wasn't until the 2000s that Irmscher, now 70, began collecting Gennett memorabilia. "When I started out, I thought, I'll just concentrate on sound effects records because that's my dad. Then I was exposed to the Black Patti 78s, which I loved. That's still my favorite, with the beautiful label. Pretty soon I was collecting anything related to Gennett or its related labels." Today she has more than 3,000 78s, all arranged in chronological order, along with a massive collection of ephemera — photographs, flyers, brochures, advertisements, odds and ends — that formed the basis of *Images of America: Gennett Records and Starr Piano.*

It has become for her a fascinating and consuming mission, one that has introduced her to collectors all over the world. Typically, she buys through eBay or one of her contacts, rarely venturing to estate sales or flea markets. The family name is not always helpful in these transactions, however.

"Sometimes I'll say who I am. I don't do it right off the bat, because that can work for or against you. My friends know who I am and treat me fairly, but some collectors think, 'she must really want this, so she's going to have to pay a lot more for it.' You either love collecting or it drives you crazy."

Keeping History Alive

Rick Kennedy was 24 years old when he took a job as a journalist for the *Richmond Palladium-Item* newspaper in the early 1980s. A music major in college, he was aware of the city's history and, he says, "I was captivated by the fact that I was living within walking distance of the Starr Piano site along the river. I could throw a rock from my apartment to the train depot. It amazed

Starr Piano company

"My mother would get calls from Japan or Europe, someone wanting to know about Gennett Records. Could they come and touch the ground where those records were made? My sister and I thought it was weird."

Linda Gennett Irmscher

me that that's where those guys came in from Chicago — Louis Armstrong and King Oliver. I used to take friends down and drink beer in the Starr Valley. It was really nasty looking back there, nothing like it is now. Very few people cared anything about it."

By then the vast Starr Piano compound was in ruins. Once encompassing nearly 40 buildings in the gorge, by the time Kennedy had his first beer at the site there were only a handful remaining. Most were demolished in the 1970s, the others left to crumble. A fire in the 1990s destroyed much of the original Starr building, although it left the Gennett Records logo — a painting of a parrot perched on a 78 record — intact. "In 1980," he says, "you

had no idea that Gennett Records ever existed."

In some ways it is an American story, similar to those of small cities all over the Midwest, industrial communities that flourished for decades before slowly and painfully winding down, both population and civic pride shriveling as factories closed or moved overseas. There are towns similar to Richmond all over Indiana, but few of their stories feature such a remarkable cast of characters, even if most of them were walk-on parts. Where else can you find so many artists getting their first recording experiences, making their first impressions, taking their first tentative steps toward changing the world one

note at a time?

Fortunately, the Gennett story does not end in rubble and ruin. Despite decades of neglect, the legacy of Starr Piano and its record label has been revitalized by locals and non-locals alike, obsessives who love the music and the legends.

The Starr-Gennett Foundation was set up in the early 1990s to preserve and promote the history around Richmond and beyond. Under its direction, the Starr Piano site was rehabbed, and the remaining structures — part of the main Gennett building and half of a smokestack — were reinforced. Today there's a park there, usually full of joggers, bicyclists, and music fans. It's also the site of the Walk of Fame, a

series of large mosaic medallions set into the walking path, featuring portraits of some of the most famous musicians who recorded in Richmond.

The Starr-Gennett Foundation started that project in 2007, adding new honorees every year or so. After so many years in the ground, however, the medallions are starting to weather and crack. Remarkably, very few have faded; their colors remain vibrant despite the constant exposure. "Those medallions can't handle the weather," says Kennedy. "They're going to have to dig those babies up. But I don't think they'll have any trouble finding places in town to put them. They're beautiful, and a lot of the businesses would love to have them in storefronts."

"Sometimes," says Irmscher, "I think there's more interest in Gennett around the world. The people actually living in Richmond have moved past it or aren't aware of it." With Irmscher as its vice president, the Starr-Gennett Foundation is working to correct that, and one of its most successful programs involves outreach into local and regional schools with lesson plans and field trips to tour the surviving buildings and listen to jazz musicians play those old songs. "We're hoping they tell the parents all about it," she says. "We're hoping that's the way to make sure this history survives. They need to know. It's part of the history of their city."

And then there are the murals — a less concerted effort but an effective one. Every building seems to have at least one exterior wall painted, which turns the city into something like a museum exhibition. Turn a corner and you might see Lonnie Johnson walking out of a wall, Hoagy Carmichael staring down at traffic, Bix Beiderbecke & His Rhythm Jugglers presiding over the patio at Firehouse Barbecue, an unidentified bluesman peeking out of a window down the alley from Blockhead Records, or Charley Patton staring quizzically from that green-blue brick wall. There is something truly otherworldly about these images, which allow these musicians to haunt the town like benevolent ghosts, constantly reminding the present of the past that cannot be left behind. ∎

BOY FROM THE NORTH COUNTRY

Digging into Bob Dylan's roots

By Anne Margaret Daniel

"I'M NORTH DAKOTA-Minnesota Midwestern. I'm that color. I speak that way. I'm from someplace called the Iron Range. My brains and feelings have come from there."
— Bob Dylan, *Playboy,* 1966

Born in St. Mary's Hospital in Duluth, Minnesota, on May 24, 1941, Robert Allen Zimmerman lived in that small port city, tucked into the westernmost finger of Lake Superior, until he was six, when his family moved to Hibbing. The towns scattered along the lakeshore near Duluth, clinging to the waters of the lake and to Highway 61, have names from settlement times, Native American languages, and the French and Indian War: Knife River, Beaver Bay, Grand Marais, Castle Danger. The great lake itself was called gitchi-gami, or great sea, by the Ojibwe or Chippewa people who were living there before European explorers, fur trappers, and settlers arrived.

In downtown Duluth, a stocky gray statue of Leif Erikson gazes out over the waters of the lake that poet Henry Wadsworth Longfellow called Gitche Gumee in his poem "Hiawatha." Erikson's likeness was erected to commemorate the possibility that Vikings sailed to Duluth from Norway via the great lake, sometime around 1000 A.D. Indeed, in 1926, a replica Viking

longship made that voyage successfully.

Whether or not the Vikings were there centuries earlier, Minnesota — named by the indigenous Dakota people — was settled in the 1800s by immigrants from cold, northern European countries: Norwegians, as Erikson was, and Swedes. In 1966, Bob Dylan humorously claimed this heritage, announcing to an interviewer in Stockholm, "I happen to be a Swede myself."

Later, in his autobiography *Chronicles Vol. 1* (2004), Dylan recalled hearing Harry Truman speak in the shadow of the Erikson statue; he wrote, too, about hearing Buddy Holly at the Duluth National Guard Armory when he was a teenager, just days before Holly's untimely death. History, legend, rhetoric, music: Dylan's deepest-running roots began here. And, as he wrote in *Chronicles,* he was not isolated or cut off from anything in Minnesota. Instead, he felt he could get anywhere from there. "Highway 61, the main thoroughfare of the country blues," he wrote, "begins about where I came from ... Duluth to be exact. I always felt like I'd started on it, always had been on it, and could go anywhere from it[.]"

Most accounts of Dylan as a musician, including his own first chapter in *Chronicles Vol. 1*, begin when he came east to New York City in the bitter cold

January of 1961. Cold? Yes. "[B]ut I'd started out from the frostbitten North Country," he wrote, "a little corner of the earth where the dark frozen woods and icy roads didn't faze me."

Shortly after he arrived in New York, Dylan went to the Café Wha? on MacDougal Street and owner Manny Roth let the 19-year-old play some Woody Guthrie songs. By that October, Dylan had made such a name for himself that John Hammond of Columbia Records signed him to a contract. In his autobiography, Dylan recounts the interview he gave at that time to Billy James, Columbia's head of publicity, which is believed to be the first surviving official interview with him.

Apart from not seeing himself at the time "like anybody," Dylan wrote that the rest of the interview "was pure hokum," that wonderful American carnival word that goes along with bunkum, hogwash, or hooey for what ain't necessarily so. Yet when it comes to what that word tells about Bobby Zimmerman, Bob Dylan, and the Midwest, the interview isn't hokum at all.

Golden Chords

It was James Gatz who had been loafing along the beach that afternoon in a torn green jersey and a pair of canvas pants, but it was already Jay Gatsby who borrowed a rowboat, pulled out to the Tuolomee, and informed Cody that a wind might catch him and break him up in half an hour.

— F. Scott Fitzgerald,
The Great Gatsby (1925)

Hibbing is not far from Duluth, but it is no seaport town — a major difference — and has no highway stretching from the cold northern start of the country, down the length of Mark Twain's Mississippi, to the gulfmouth of the Delta Blues. But Dylan's mother's family lived in the area, and Bob attended grade school and high school here.

During that interview with Columbia publicist Billy James in 1961, though, Dylan veered through honesty and, indeed, into palpable hokum about Hibbing. "For the most part," he told James, "my base has been in upper — way upper — Minnesota. Almost to the border. ... Hibbing, Minnesota — that's a mining town — lumber town."

In the same interview, Dylan claimed he first ran away from home at age seven and joined a traveling carnival at 13. Where did he go? "All around the Midwest, uh, Gallup, New Mexico, then to Texas, and then ... ." The citation of New Mexico as the Midwest is almost as funny as Jay Gatsby telling Nick Carraway that his "Middle West" hometown is San Francisco. Yet Dylan confesses to having graduated from high school in Hibbing, and having spent most of his time there from age "seven to seventeen." This is entirely true. He got his first guitar in Hibbing, and put together his first bands there. At Crippa Music on East Howard Street, he bought his sheet music and records. At the Lybba Theater on First Avenue, owned by his uncles and named for his great-grandmother, he saw the movies of the 1950s. He was on a bowling team called the Gutter Boys and had a beautiful blond girlfriend named Echo Helstrom. Her mother, Martha, told biographer Anthony Scaduto in 1972 that

Bob had wanted to be like Elvis Presley.

With guitarist Monte Edwardson and drummer LeRoy Hoikkala, Dylan had a high school band called the Golden Chords. In a 1999 piece for the unauthorized Bob Dylan magazine *On the Tracks,* Hoikkala told interviewer Lars Lindh the name arrived naturally. "Bob ... could really chord with the piano and the guitar, really chord beautifully," Hoikkala recalled. "He was really a natural at chording. And my drums were gold, sparkling gold. So, we said Golden ... Chords, that's how we got the name."

Hoikkala went on, explaining how the boys "used to sit together with a reel-to-reel tape recorder at night and tape the AM stations that came in really good at night ... and then Bob would play them, because that was more the type of songs that he liked; the bluesy songs."

But as for writing songs, Hoikkala's answer is the best statement on Dylan's early career as a folksinger, and as a rock and roller, you'll ever read:

He changed a lot of songs. He listened to a song and he changed them. He didn't like the way they read. Just like a lot of the songs that he's recorded. I [used] to say that he wasn't copying someone, but he took the basic song and if he didn't like the lyrics he just changed it to what he wanted. He was a natural. He is a great songwriter. Some songs he didn't change, others he changed to his own liking.

Thus, before Dylan had ever left Hibbing, before he went to Duluth and began playing and learning about jazz, before he arrived in Minneapolis for college and started calling himself Bob Dillon (or Dylan), before he heard a Woody Guthrie record, the integral elements of his creative personality — collector, singer, musician, and songwriter — were already in place.

Soaking up Sounds

On a Friday night in November 2002,

veteran folk and roots music revivalists Koerner, Ray & Glover played what would be their last concert at Princeton University. Dave "Snaker" Ray had been diagnosed that year with lung cancer, and he died a week later, on Thanksgiving Day. In a small performance space in the music department, with superb acoustics and less than 200 people in attendance for the free show, the three men made a gorgeous evening of the blues, rags, and hollers they had played together, off and on, for the past 40 years and more.

Ray was quietly gracious, smiling often, handling his guitar with competence and care. You wouldn't have known how ill he was that night. He was joined, as ever, by Tony "Little Sun" Glover, a rock critic and harmonica genius who taught Mick Jagger how to play blues harp, and "Spider" John Koerner, whom he'd met way back when at the University of Minnesota. The trio had held a mighty influence on Dylan when he arrived in Minneapolis. He had meant to study at the university, but instead found his schooling in the coffeehouses and clubs of the Dinkytown district and the folk record collections of friends.

"[Dylan] was like a sponge, interested in everything," recalled Ray, who introduced numerous people — including a young Bob Dylan — to the music of Lead Belly, Big Bill Broonzy, and Lightnin' Hopkins.

As Koerner remembered, Dylan stood out even then for "certain qualities that made him one-up on the rest of us. He had a certain kind of confidence and [he would] write things you could see had something to them."

Dylan, Koerner, and Ray shared songs, books, records, and instruments so frequently that, at a 2007 exhibition of Dylan artifacts from his Minnesota life — or lives — Koerner laughed over a guitar in a case. "This guitar here," he told Minnesota Public Radio, "it looks like my old guitar."

But years earlier, as early as 1956, Dylan had recorded some cover songs with friends. The earliest known surviving tape, of him recording and talking with his friend John Bucklen, was made in the Zimmermans' home in early 1958; the fragments have been released in various documentaries, as have parts of a tape he made with another pal, Ric Kangas. Dylan's first long recorded session, however, was in May 1960 in St. Paul, Minnesota, after two sisters, Karen and Terri Wallace, heard him sing at a place called the Purple Onion.

According to Terri, Dylan wanted to listen to himself. On the bootlegged tape, she explains, "He had never heard how he sounded before. And he knew he was gonna go to New York" — to find Woody Guthrie, and to make a name for himself as a singer-songwriter.

The tape opens with Paul Clayton's "Gotta Travel On," includes many songs by Guthrie, and concludes with "Payday at Coal Creek." Various excerpts have long been available — including on the appropriately named "Armpit Tape," allegedly recorded on a tape recorder concealed in an armpit when Karen Wallace Moynihan played the original tape to a prospective buyer years later. Bonnie Beecher, Dylan's girlfriend who would later come to New York too (and marry Dylan's friend Hugh Romney, entertainment director at the Gaslight Café and known since 1969 as Wavy Gravy), recorded more of Dylan's covers of traditional songs later in 1960 at her Minneapolis home. The "Minnesota Hotel Tape" remains the standout in the early Minnesota Dylan recordings that gave rise to the first bootleg in the music world, *Great White Wonder* (1969).

Soon Dylan would meet Woody Guthrie and write him a song; he would become close friends with Paul Clayton and learn hundreds of traditional songs and arrangements from the man he remembers as "an intellectual, a scholar, and a romantic with an encyclopedic knowledge of balladry." But Dylan's passion for music, the stories his songs told, the sound of the voices and the guitars from the flat-picked to the symphonic 12-stringed, began in Minnesota. Literally — he took it from there.

Native Sons

Thought I'd shaken the wonder
and the phantoms of my youth
Rainy days on the Great Lakes,
walkin' the hills of old Duluth.
— Bob Dylan,
"Something There Is About You," 1973

Dylan has never shaken off the Midwest, and particularly Minnesota, and seems happy not to have done so. As his music tours have rolled through the decades, he's always been certain to schedule dates throughout the heartland of America: Chicago, Cincinnati, Dayton, Iowa City, East Lansing, St. Louis, Carbondale, and Minneapolis and Duluth.

He and his brother quietly purchased the Orpheum Theater in Minneapolis when it was in danger of being torn down and returned it to being a thriving venue. He owned for decades, and perhaps still owns, ranchland in rural Minnesota. He wrote many of the songs for *Blood on the Tracks* (1975) there, and recorded some of the tracks in Minneapolis in the winter of 1974 with a group of local musicians and a 1930s Martin from the Podium Guitar Shop, which had opened near the university in 1959, the year Dylan first arrived.

To conclude the first volume of his autobiography, Dylan brings it all back home. A baseball fan who has played some of his most intimate and excellent shows since 2004 in ballparks — and who enjoyed a visit to the Baseball Hall of Fame after a 2006 show at Doubleday Field — Dylan wrote of Roger Maris breaking Babe Ruth's home run record, which took place in October 1961, just as Dylan was signing with Hammond and Columbia.

"Maris was from Hibbing, Minnesota, of all places," he wrote, then listed other Minnesotans "that I felt akin to." There was Charles Lindbergh of Little Falls; F. Scott Fitzgerald, author of *The Great Gatsby* and a descendant of the man who wrote "The Star-Spangled Banner," of St. Paul; Eddie Cochrane of Albert Lea, "one of the early rock-and-roll geniuses"; and Sinclair Lewis, who "won the Nobel Prize for Literature, the first American to do so." Lewis, Dylan wrote, "had written *Elmer Gantry* and was the master of absolute realism, had invented it. He was from Sauk Centre."

Then Dylan, who now is the latest American to win the Nobel Prize for Literature, celebrated his fellows and sang a song of himself:

Native sons — adventurers, prophets, writers, and musicians. They were all from the North Country. Each one followed their own vision, didn't care what the pictures showed. Each one of them would have understood what my inarticulate dreams were about. I felt like I was one of them or all of them put together.

Those "inarticulate dreams" are straight out of *Gatsby* — as is the "all of them put together." When Nick Carraway speaks to Gatsby for the last time, he pays him the only compliment he ever uttered to Gatsby's face: "You're worth the whole damn bunch put together."

As he began his career in New York City, Dylan styled himself as a composite of Minnesota's most celebrated native sons. He stood with them, inheriting not just their musical mantle but specifically their literary laurels. The trajectory was, as present-day events have borne out, truer than he might have known in 1961, or 2004. However, with Dylan you have to wonder whether he might just have been confident of everything to come all along, back in those earliest Midwest days, in his younger and more vulnerable years. His Minnesota roots and self-characterization as a man of the heartland puts a powerful focus on where he comes from as integral to Dylan's career, rather than on the much-discussed many thousand miles he's traveled, and those to come as he goes traveling on. ∎

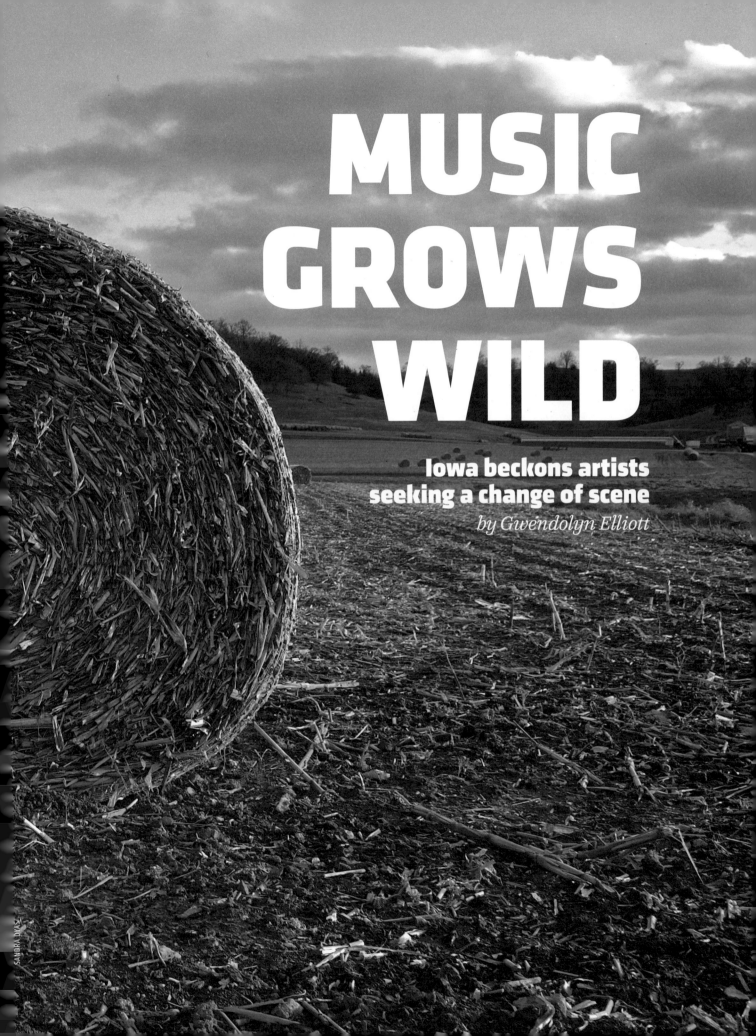

MUSIC GROWS WILD

Iowa beckons artists seeking a change of scene

by Gwendolyn Elliott

Jesse Sykes

ESSE SYKES DOESN'T HAVE A smart device or a laptop. Her phone is an eight-year-old flip phone she says was "dropped in my dog Ruby's water bowl and it still works fine." When visiting Seattle, as she does regularly to collaborate with her musical partner Phil Wandscher, one-half of her band the Sweet Hereafter, she borrows the computer of her 83-year-old mother, who still lives in the city.

It's during one such visit, as she is wrapping recording on the follow-up to her critically acclaimed 2011 album, *Marble Son,* that she sits at a corner table in the Ballard Smoke Shop and I step in out of the rain to meet her. Wandscher is there with her: He's not only Sykes' ex-boyfriend and most-enduring creative collaborator, he's also somewhat of a chauffeur when she's in town, as Sykes also doesn't drive.

"He calls it Driving Miss Daisy," Sykes says, with a resigned half-chuckle, as if she's explained the arrangement before. Wandscher is unamused. "Why don't you two talk for a while?" he says, and heads to the bar.

I'm struck by the familial ease between them — somewhat sibling-like and antagonistic, yet chummy. This is notable, as the pair share a tangled history: a ten-year-long, ultimately failed romance that miraculously didn't kill the band on its way out.

I've met Sykes before — she used to contribute essays to *Seattle Weekly,* the alt-weekly newspaper where I used to work — though it's been a few years. She is now 49, and whether it's good genes or the farm-fresh Iowa air, she has somehow managed not to age. Her long,

straight hair is still jet-black; her unique Southwestern-goth look, which gathers together chunky silver jewelry, blue jeans, and black platform shoes, is still intact.

Finding a Refuge

Sykes has lived in Ames, Iowa, since 2010. Her decision to uproot from her Seattle home of 20 years to America's heartland was, in fact, a matter of the heart: "I moved to Iowa because I fell in love," she wrote in a 2012 essay.

There are other factors, too. Like a nagging feeling she would live there someday, formed on a train trip she once took with her mother from New York to Colorado.

In that same essay, she writes; "I remember the first state we rode across that made me feel truly far from home, far enough away from my comfort zone to wonder what it would be like to 'be from here.' 'Here' seemed like nowhere, just a small cluster of lights — sometimes just a single light shining like a lantern on the horizon. The train was an invisible whistling force, and it was just the two of us — inside the darkness — passing through Iowa.

"Had you told me in that moment that I would someday live there," she continues, "I would have been thrilled. All that distance and space would have set well with me then — far from home, the mystery, and my God, you had to cross the great Mississippi to get there."

It was a similar motivation to "get away" that led Sykes to Seattle, a formative move in her young creative life. As she puts it, "getting to Iowa is my version of [my Seattle story] as an adult."

"When I came to Seattle in '90, it was to disappear," she says. She was 22 years old, a recent graduate of the prestigious Rhode Island School of Design with a BFA in photography. She spent a few months in New York, which she says changed her. "I realized it wasn't my world. If I was to stay among a lot of those people, my soul would be destroyed."

"I had seen the movie *Streetwise,*" she says, of photographer Mary Ellen Mark and filmmaker Martin Bell's gritty 1984 documentary about Seattle's street kids. "I became pretty obsessed with that movie, I wanted to be a street photographer. Seattle, through that lens, looked like a gritty, forlorn place where you could disappear."

But Sykes was developing a persona that was hard to ignore. She began playing in country-folk outfit Hominy with her then-husband Jim Sykes. When the band and marriage fizzled, and Wandscher's Whiskeytown disbanded in 1999, the two guitarists linked up and formed the Sweet Hereafter.

The band slowly began to take off. Its Tucker Martine-produced debut, *Reckless Burning,* a gentle, smoldering, collection of country noir, was well-received. Shortly after, they signed to Barsuk, the label that put out the group's next two albums, 2004's *Oh, My Girl,* and 2007's *Like, Love, Lust and the Open Halls of the Soul,* both also produced by Martine. (*No Depression* called *Oh, My Girl* "languid, ethereal, and spiced with echoey forebodings just this side of spaghetti-western twang." Of *Like, Love, Lust* it noted: "[Jesse Sykes is] strong-willed, idiosyncratic, and charismatic.")

The Sweet Hereafter began touring a lot, grew a fan base in Europe, and

"People are really forgetting the importance of being human, observing other humans, taking in your space, feeling your space, and being in the moment. It sounds so small, but it's so important."

Jesse Sykes

started to collaborate with bands on the fringes — and beyond — of roots music: drone metal and experimental groups like Earth, Boris, and Sunn O))). It was this new, expanded sound that debuted on *Marble Son,* the best example of what Sykes calls the "spectral" vision of the Sweet Hereafter, and such a leap forward in tone it seemed to be the one poised to align all the elements — a robust and diverse fan base, good label support (this time via Station Grey/ Fargo Records), and a band that gelled like never before.

Wandscher and Sykes had broken up by this time, and shortly after *Marble Son* was released, two key members of the band departed. The shift was difficult for Sykes. She had been visiting Iowa frequently to visit her then-boyfriend (now fiancé), and decided to move there, re-configuring the Sweet Hereafter to the duo it has remained since.

The relationship of Iowa, where many of *Marble Son's* songs were written, to that particular period of her life, she says, was that Iowa "saved me by giving me that solace and that protective feeling [from the many changes to the band]."

Now a resident for six years, Sykes speaks as lovingly of her adopted home as she once did about the Pacific Northwest.

"I love the space, and I love the vastness," she says. "Iowa is so pastoral and beautiful, all the things people say about it are true. When you get off the highway, there really are these stunning little groves, these bastions of tranquility. I sound like a fundamentalist, but it looks like heaven. The prairie, before it was decimated — you can find remnants [of

what it was]. ... If you could see it, these acres and acres of natural prairie, I would argue they're even more beautiful than the mountains out [West]."

Sykes has adapted to life in Iowa and gets by with a mortgage most Seattle homeowners would kill for, but Iowa has also adapted to her needs. She often uses the state as a metaphor for her many expansive ideas about life and beyond. Iowa is, she writes, "The state with almost no wilderness to be had, but endless space — space that forces you to find the wilderness within — the state that you need to get down inside of to see and appreciate for its incredible pockets of beauty."

The pace of life in that state is also just slow and quiet enough that there's less struggle with the frenzy of urban life that's always a consideration, for example, in ever-bustling Seattle. Like so many other cities, Seattle is experiencing rapid growth and encroaching technology on a scale she's not all that comfortable with.

"It feels like an assault to me," she says. "It takes work to remain engaged and not shut down emotionally. People are really forgetting the importance of being human, observing other humans, taking in your space, feeling your space, and being in the moment. It sounds so small, but it's so important."

Openness and Olive Garden

Meanwhile, elsewhere in Iowa, singer-songwriter Lissie is enjoying her view. "I am looking out at dry cornfields and trees with some good colors. A lot of leaves have fallen in the last week, so it

feels like it's transitioning, which I am enjoying because I was in Southern California for 12 years. The change of weather was something that I missed."

Lissie, born Elisabeth Maurus, is on the phone from her farmhouse — she won't say exactly where — and, other than the occasional terrifying thought or two ("I'm probably going to have to get a shotgun," she admits), she is settling in just fine after moving here a year ago.

Her personality is breezy and doesn't hold back — something which, for better or worse, got her expelled from high school, but likely also expedited her career.

Lissie was raised in Rock Island, Illinois, part of the Quad Cities region that's comprised of four counties in Southeastern Iowa and Northwest Illinois, near the Mississippi River. At 32, the singer-songwriter has lived in Colorado, Paris, and California, toured extensively throughout Europe, the US, and Australia, and now has three studio albums to her name. Her music falls somewhere between roots-rock and pure pop, starring the singer's clean, confident vocals that sound alternately like Margo Timmons and Lana Del Rey.

Her new 10-acre property is a world of change from her last seven years in Ojai, California, and the five she spent in L.A. before that. Those 12 years in California and her return to the Midwest are the subject of her latest album, *My Wild West*. The video for its first single, "Don't You Give Up On Me," was filmed at the farmhouse. She calls the tune "a plea to God — or to a person, or to whomever — to hang in there with me while I figure it out."

Lissie

Lissie says she reached a point in California when "I was like, I miss my family, I miss the seasons, I miss the Midwest. I always had this romanticized dream, since I was young, of someday owning a farm in Iowa. It went from being this daydream to being like, well, actually, I could probably afford that. [With the money] I'm paying in rent in California, I could easily buy a farm in Iowa. So I just went and looked at some properties. I think artists in this day and age, if you have a fan base and you can tour, and be busy creating content you can post online, then you aren't obligated to live anywhere in particular."

Though there was the emotional, umbilical pull of being closer to home, Lissie's dream of owning a farm in Iowa went way back to before she ever left Illinois. "I spent half my life going across the [Centennial] bridge to Iowa," she says. "The Olive Garden is in Iowa, and I loved the Olive Garden."

This is the second time in months that the topic of the Olive Garden is brought up, without irony, by an artist I've been interviewing. It first came up when I spoke with singer-songwriter

Tom Brosseau earlier this year, who, similar to Sykes and Lissie, has relocated from L.A. to the center of the country. In his case, he's returned to his home state of North Dakota.

Brosseau happens to be friends with 90-year-old *Grand Forks Herald* columnist Marilyn Hagerty, whose 2012 review of the local Olive Garden went viral. His song "Stuck on the Roof Again" is about her, and they occasionally meet for dinner or a beer. "Marilyn is not afraid to drink a beer," he told me. (After our interview, Brosseau sent me a signed copy of *Hagerty's Grand Forks: A History of American Dining in 128 Reviews*. It included a note from him with the words, "It's so important to be local.")

Lissie shares a similar view. "I am only a few hours from family, so I'm close enough to be part of family dinners and everyone's important events, but I also have my own little nook," she says, "People here are really friendly and helpful, maybe a little nosy, but with good intentions.

"I think family is really important," she adds. "Being part of a cooperative network of people is important ...

[because especially] in Northern areas, people have to live through hard winters. In small towns, people are very interconnected."

She gets specific, citing her Iowa friends as an example of this small-town interconnectedness and its inherent diversity. "One [of my friends is] a stay-at-home mom, one's an emergency room nurse, one's a parole officer. Having people not living in the bubble of the [entertainment] industry, it was nice to get back into the real world. I mean, yeah, what I do is interesting, but it's not any more important than what anyone else does. I think people can take themselves way too seriously in the entertainment world."

Further, she adds, "There have been no challenges, really. I am probably missing out on some daily opportunities, but I have been touring all year and I am only a few hours from an airport that can get me anywhere I need to go. ... I'm setting up a little studio in my house so hopefully I can figure out how I can record and get work done here. With the internet, I can just send the files to the mixer and they can just email me back

the mixed song and I didn't have to leave the house. I didn't even have to get out of my pajamas. Technology makes it easier."

Connecting to What's Real

In a business that places so much emphasis on networks, connections, and "who you know," a move to the Midwest could still be risky for an independent musician. There are, however, a growing number of artists like Sykes, Lissie, and Brosseau who just don't care, and there are clear success stories when you factor in the work of record labels like Indiana's Secretly Canadian and Omaha, Nebraska's Saddle Creek Records. There are vibrant music scenes in places like Iowa City, home to Iris DeMent and Greg Brown, and similar scenes elsewhere.

But, at least for now, the biggest draw for Lissie has to do with what artists in bigger cities often can't do: spread out and reconnect.

"For me, [the move] was to be closer to family and to be somewhere I could afford to own land — not just a house — to be exposed to a more realistic sample of the population, and to cultivate some of my other interests," she says. Those interests include preserving her property in its natural state, getting a garden together, and maybe even starting a hobby farm.

She is excited about the possibilities. "Once I've owned any tillable acreage for more than a year, I'll be eligible to go into a government program and get paid to not farm. I just want to set up my land for conservancy — for birds, bees, and butterflies. They have special seed blends for different kinds of flowers that attract different kinds of pollinators. The state offers all kinds of resources and the University of Iowa has an extension office [to help] you put your land into conservancy so it just grows wild." ∎

BELIEVE-LAND

A roots music renaissance simmers just under the surface in Northeast Ohio

by Jay Minkin

Brent Kirby

"The music scene in Northeast Ohio is not only full of talented musicians and songwriters, but good-hearted people who are supportive and encouraging. It's sometimes like a sibling rivalry in a good way, where you push each other to make everyone better."

John Patrick Halling

LAST YEAR THE NATIONAL spotlight shined on Cleveland, Ohio, as the city hosted two professional sports championship series and a major political convention within the span of five months. But it wasn't just those big events that breathed new life into this Rust Belt town. It took years of perseverance, strategic planning, investments, and a positive outlook to change the perception of the aging industrial city into the jewel that now sits on the shores of Lake Erie.

That blueprint was duplicated just beyond the Cuyahoga County border in places like Akron, home of the Goodyear Blimp, and Kent, where Kent State University and new large businesses have spurred growth. It helped that a few great ambassadors — Chef Michael Symon, NBA star LeBron James, and musicians like the Black Keys, Chrissie Hynde, and Patrick Sweany — helped define the gritty landscape and amplify the cultural value of Northeast Ohio.

These days, at Brothers Wine Bar in Cleveland, Brent Kirby helms a thriving music community as he hosts something he calls 10x3, a scheduled weekly format that allows 10 songwriters to perform two originals and one cover song apiece. A working musician himself, Kirby can be found playing nightly solo or with his numerous bands: Brent Kirby & His Luck, the hard rocking Jack Fords, or his monthly ensemble The New Soft Shoe, which pulls its material from the Gram Parsons songbook. He also regularly jams with some of the area's finest musicians, including local keyboardist "Maestro" Chris Hanna and pedal steel master "Reverend" Al Moss.

"For the most part, the musicians in Cleveland are not trying to fit a norm of the industry structure," says Kirby. He adds that the city is "bubbling with amazing and talented folks who are comingling within a great networking community."

Another full-time musician who has embraced Cleveland's networking culture is Thor Platter, who moved here from Buffalo, New York, in 2008. In his bluegrass trio, Platter has aligned himself with two local luminaries in bassist Paul Lewis and banjoist Paul Kovac, who both have taught him invaluable vocal technique. In what once seemed to be a very competitive atmosphere, Platter has found a positive camaraderie among fellow players and a valuable support system. "I don't understand why Cleveland can't be more in the national spotlight" he says. "I fell in love with Ohio and it's a great home base to tour around from."

Among the new wave of notable musicians is the jangly explosiveness of John Patrick & the Outside Voices. Typical in these parts, John Patrick Halling — a charismatic performer — attended Kent State University then soon found work in a warehouse, which helped him pay the rent. Meanwhile, he started hitting the open mics in 2013 and began working his way through Cleveland's music world. For his 2015 album *Boy in the Water,* he brought in some friends to round out his sound, and the group came out of those sessions as a real band. Incidentally, their first live gig was at one of Kirby's 10x3 shows.

Halling had already gotten to know guitarists Jimmy Dykes and Johnny Miller, bassist Kevin McManus, and drummer Sam Langstaff as they played in other bands. "The music scene in Northeast Ohio is not only full of talented musicians and songwriters," he explains, "but good-hearted people who are supportive and encouraging. It's sometimes like a sibling rivalry in a good way, where you push each other to make everyone better."

After building some momentum, Halling and his band traveled to Amish Electric Chair Studios to record their debut album. Nicknamed "The Crush Factory," the studio's three rooms — designed for both live and multi-track recording — are built around a hand-made oak mastering desk in the control room. Halling and his band camped on the studio's four acres of hillside in Athens, Ohio, and captured the energy of their surroundings on their self-funded album *Hound Dogs,* which was released in January 2017.

The artistic energy and independent

Gretchen Pleuss

spirit of groups like Halling's band — all in their mid-20s — is a testament to the simmering possibilities in and around Cleveland these days.

A Tight-Knit Community

Another group making fast strides in the city is the Gage Brothers, who have gone from playing open mics to playing premier area clubs like the Beachland Ballroom & Tavern, Music Box Supper Club, Happy Dog, and the GAR Hall — all of which are well-known stops for national touring artists

Older brother Ben Gage (harmonica, cajón) and his younger brother Zach (guitar) were playing music at church and began practicing folk songs afterward at home. This led to the duo performing in Akron at open mics and taverns in 2014, eventually breaking into Cleveland's music network a year later.

One night, local mandolinist Brendan O'Malley was tending bar at a tavern where the brothers were performing and happened to have his instrument with him. The trio started performing together and was joined at one gig by singer-songwriter Chris Volpe, who added banjo and pedal steel — what proved to be the finishing touch to their sound.

All four members of the Gage Brothers sing, layering their vocal harmonies together like something created in the back kitchen of Melt Bar & Grilled, the famed local chain known for its gourmet grilled cheese sandwiches.

"As area musicians become aware of each other," notes Ben Gage, "it helps to get feedback on strengths and weaknesses. The community is now a tight-knit group, and Cleveland is a very cool place to make music. Venue owners and others who support the working

musicians are helping make our talents more known."

The foursome are releasing their self-titled second full-length record this spring with 11 original tunes and one cover of the traditional song "No More Auction Block for Me." The disc includes guest player Kevin Martinez, who has played with Akron's The Speedbumps, and local favorite Roger Hoover, whom the Brothers brought in to play bass. One song in particular that's worth a listen is "Caged." It tells a story about a coal miner who carries a bird into the mine with him, not just to hope it continues singing, but also to remind him of what there is in the world worth loving.

Peer Group

"It's amazing how many people in the same age group are inspiring each other," says singer-songwriter Gretchen Pleuss.

Roger Hoover

"There is a communal feel amongst artists, stimulating growth and inspiration."

A college graduate with a degree in anthropology, Pleuss has been writing songs since the age of 12 and rounded out her education with classical guitar and piano courses. Last fall she moved from the rural farmlands of Wooster, Ohio, to Akron not only to be closer to performance spaces, but also to surround herself with creative professionals and artists. She works what she refers to as "odds and ends" — assorted jobs like waitressing and seasonal freight shipping — while focusing on her musical path. Her influences include the phrasing, jazz rhythms, and songwriting style of Joni Mitchell as well as genre-bending women songwriters from the '90s.

Her 2016 release *From Birth, to Breath, to Bone* was a self-produced labor of love cut to vinyl and CD. Several musicians lent a hand, recording layers of sound to support Pleuss' sweet vocals. She wrote the signature track "Waves Like Drums" after she returned from a two-week tour of Ireland, while she was still reminiscing about the natural landscapes and folklore. The song captures her fingerpicking style as well as her tuned-down guitar within an experimental composition. She's planning a more stripped-down album highlighting her guitar and vocal work later this year.

This song-centrism pervades the Northeast Ohio music scene, where singer-songwriters anchor much of the community. Veteran singer-songwriter/pianist Rachel Brown spends her days teaching music at a local high school. At night, she slips into her polka-dot dress, places a flower in her hair, and takes the stage to the delight of her adoring audience. "I just love the dresses of the '50s and '60s," she explains, "and they say you can't be sad when you're wearing polka dots."

Like many in the Cleveland area's scene of deep roots, Brown's family encompasses multiple generations of musicians, from her parents and aunts to her two children — both of whom performed in Cleveland's celebrated Contemporary Youth Orchestra. Brown grew up listening to gospel at church, since rock and roll was forbidden in a home that only played George, Merle, Patsy, and Loretta records. These days, her musical interests are more varied, and she draws crowds whether she's playing with locals or artists dropping in from out of town. A recent show placed her on a shared bill with Nashville's Brandy Clark, where the two discussed how difficult the singer-songwriter career path is and how it's either "feast or famine."

'Give What You Get Back'

One local artist who has found his 15 minutes of national fame is guitarist and songwriter Roger Hoover. "What transformed into the Americana and alt-country phenomenon was very much happening in Kent with folks playing Brady's Café or the Kent State Folk Festival," explains Hoover, formerly of national touring Ohio roots bands the Magpies and the Whiskeyhounds. "Attending songwriting workshops during the folk festival conferences and learning the history of roots music is something that left an imprint on me.

"The scene in Northeast Ohio is exploding with so much unique talent," he adds, "Now, I'm sharing my knowledge and hard-learned lessons with the next generation because I'm so grateful for the folks who helped me."

When he was invited to play a house party in Conway, Arkansas, Hoover developed a friendship with the man who invited him, Matt White. White introduced him to Travis Hill, owner of Last Chance Records, who signed Hoover to the label with the release of his 2016 album *Pastures*. Hill brought the band back to Arkansas to perform at the Whitewater Tavern (coincidentally owned by White) in Little Rock. He also made a vinyl pressing to send with Hoover on a tour of Europe this spring, where he's working on building new audiences.

One song from the record, "Give What You Get Back," is very passionate, motivating, and karmic for Hoover. The song is based on a conversation he had with two guys at the Little Rock showcase who arrived at the club after getting off work at their blue-collar jobs. The message of the song is: "I'm here, I'm struggling, but I'm doing my best." It's about how the opportunity to reach for the American Dream the way older generations did is gone. Like many Midwesterners, Hoover struggles with that every day.

One of the players in Hoover's backing band, the Western Reserve, is guitarist Ray Flanagan, whom Brent Kirby describes as a chameleon. At 24, Flanagan can sit in and play with just about anyone in town. Hoover has been mentoring him, and in return Flanagan

has brought an incredible source of energy to Hoover's music since joining the Western Reserve. "There is no tap on his talent," boasts Hoover. "He is technically sound and doing stuff like I've never heard before. Ray is artistic, poetic, and his playing is [well] thought-out."

Indeed, Flanagan takes in the landscape and people around him, pointing out observations while touring with Hoover's band. He was so moved by protests against an oil pipeline at the Standing Rock Reservation in North Dakota that he not only researched the history of the Sioux people, but he also wrote a song titled "Plants by the Water" — a meditation on the oppression and mistreatment of indigenous people.

Though there is obviously a songwriter budding in him, for now Flanagan is content playing with Hoover and continuing to be a sponge to his bandleader's wealth of knowledge.

And that spirit of learning from one another — networking, making connections across and through the music — is the stuff on which the Cleveland area's songwriters are building a foundation. Though we locals don't want them to move out of state and have their career flourish elsewhere, we're hopeful that we can cultivate and incubate our homegrown talent within the triangle of Cleveland, Akron, and Kent. Or, as we call it, Believeland. ■

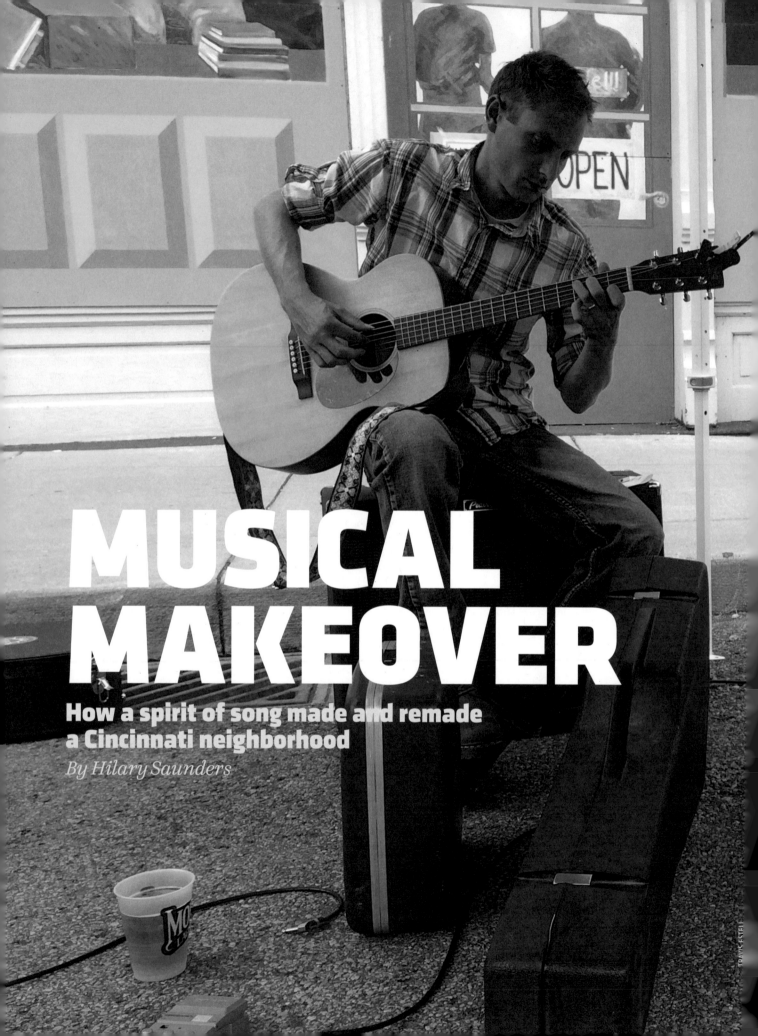

MUSICAL MAKEOVER

**How a spirit of song made and remade
a Cincinnati neighborhood**

By Hilary Saunders

Busker Elk Creek performs at Over-the-Rhine's Findlay Market.

WHEN LINFORD Detweiler moved into his Main Street apartment in Cincinnati's Over-the-Rhine neighborhood in 1989, he paid $100 a month. The third-floor walk-up in the neighborhood just north of downtown was the multi-instrumentalist and songwriter's home for almost a decade. When he and future bandmate (and wife) Karin Bergquist moved to southern Ohio after graduating from college, they heard about the neighborhood and, Detweiler says, "were really taken with that name. It just sounded so weird and magical — sort of 'Over the Rainbow' meets some unknown prince across the sea."

When the two actually visited Over-the-Rhine, Detweiler recalls their shared disbelief. In a recent interview over the phone from their current home, the Nowhere Farm, about an hour outside Cincinnati, he speaks slowly and thoughtfully. "We thought that somebody must have picked up a European city and flown it across the Atlantic Ocean and dropped it gently in the hills of Ohio, there near the Ohio River," he jokes. "We just couldn't believe it! There were blocks and blocks and blocks of these beautiful 19th-century three- and four-story brick buildings and angular streets and alleys — some of the alleys are still cobblestone. [At the time] it was very much considered the bad part of town.

"That's really where we got our start as a band and did all of our early recordings and demos — there in the bedroom overlooking Main Street. Those were really charmed days in a lot of ways," he adds, pausing in the memory. "We were just setting out as young writers, young artists, and this neighborhood was ragged and beautiful and dangerous — a lot of things we hoped our songs might be able to live up to."

Although Detweiler and Bergquist recorded their first musical demos in spring of 1989, naming their duo after their neighborhood, they didn't form a full band or release their first album, *Till We Have Faces,* until 1991. Since then, however, Over the Rhine has released 16 studio albums, attracting and retaining one of the most dedicated audiences in folk and roots music.

In the early-'90s, they were one of three major musical acts to break out of Cincinnati, alongside the grunge-inspired Afghan Whigs and alt-country group Ass Ponys. Yet within the diverse music scene of Cincinnati, which also includes a strong university district around the University of Cincinnati, Over the Rhine was the only band of national note actually living in the neighborhood Over-the-Rhine.

Jim Tarbell, a Cincinnati native, public servant, activist, former restaurant and bar owner, and all-around Over-the-Rhine neighborhood supporter, has always championed the group, both for its musicality and its homage to place. Even today, when locals of all ages and demographics see the septuagenarian on a weekday afternoon at Findlay Market — dressed stylishly in a cabbie hat, plaid waistcoat, and activist flair — they recognize him and greet him with a jolly, "Good afternoon, Mr. Tarbell!" So beloved is he in the community that there's even a three-story mural of his likeness painted on the side of a building at the intersection of Vine Street and Central Parkway.

As Detweiler remembers, Tarbell, a former city councilman and vice mayor, "came up to me at some point early in our career, almost getting down on his knees and [thanking us]. He was just over the moon that somebody had taken the name Over-the-Rhine and attached it to something positive, which was just a radical crazy idea in the early '90s."

German Flavor

The Over-the-Rhine neighborhood first came to prominence in the mid-1800s, when German immigrants began settling in greater Cincinnati. The Miami and Erie Canal used to run across Central Parkway, the street that divides downtown Cincy from Over-the-Rhine. That canal connected to the Erie Canal, which fed into the Great Lakes and eventually into the Atlantic Ocean. As the German population grew in the neighborhood, the Anglo majority on the south side of town began pejoratively referring to the community across the river as Over-the-Rhine, named for the Rhine River that flows along Germany's borders with France and Switzerland, also alluding to the negative connotation of "the other side of the tracks."

By the turn of the 20th century, the German-Americans in Over-the-Rhine began thriving. The Italianate and Queen Anne-style buildings built in the late 1800s became iconic. The growing

"We were just setting out as young writers, young artists, and this neighborhood was ragged and beautiful and dangerous — a lot of things we hoped our songs might be able to live up to."

Linford Detweiler (Over the Rhine)

brewery scene helped unite the community, and the enormous Gothic-style Music Hall, erected in 1895, served as a grand meeting place and entertainment space. In fact, the neighborhood's population at its peak in the early 20th century rose to as many as 40,000 people.

This was when music really began flourishing in Over-the-Rhine. To this day, Music Hall, which towers over the west side of the neighborhood, still hosts the Cincinnati Symphony — the fifth oldest professional orchestra in the country. Choral singing also proliferated throughout the predominantly German-American community. The Cincinnati May Festival, a two-week choir festival that still takes place annually, began in 1873, taking influence from the Saengerfests (singer festivals) of the 1840s.

As the 1900s progressed, civic assets like transportation and technology began to improve. In particular, streetcars, railways, and roads enabled greater mobility in and out of Over-the-Rhine, thus changing the predominantly German-American identity of the area. As World War II raged through the first half of the 1940s, anti-German sentiments began driving the neighborhood's German-Americans out of their homes and community.

In the following decades, like when Tarbell moved to Over-the-Rhine in 1971, the demographics shifted toward an Appalachian identity. The neighborhood's location served as a sort of crossroads between the industrial North and the South's Mason-Dixon Line,

as well as between the coastal Eastern urban centers and the Rust Belt via the Erie Canal. This all made it an easy stopping point for rural Appalachian families migrating across America.

Tarbell remembers listening to AM radio stations like WCKY and WCIN around this time, too. They would play country and gospel/soul music, respectively, in the evenings, as the signals expanded and the audiences diversified. On the ground in Over-the-Rhine, musicians like local bluegrass legend Katie Lauer (who still runs a weekly roots radio show on NPR affiliate WNKU called *Music from the Hills of Home*) led the scene.

Venues with live music boomed, as roots music poured out of the saloons along Vine Street. According to Tarbell, "Vine Street had more saloons than any street in America. Between the base of the river and the hill, [there were] somewhere between 250 and 260 saloons, or 'liquor licensees,' is the way they put it."

But while social institutions were booming, housing options began to diminish. In a misguided attempt to improve city conditions, the US Department of Housing and Urban Development (HUD) gave about $100,000 to Cincinnati to finance low-income housing for government-subsidized beneficiaries in the 1970s. Tarbell notes how, while necessary for human rights and effective city planning, the plan did not support the working class neighborhood. As a result, the diverse population of working poor was forced out of the neighborhood for those

moving into the HUD-subsidized units.

"It changed this neighborhood overnight for the worse," Tarbell opines, "because the units that became market-driven that might have attracted people of mixed use, mixed income did not become attractive because [the neighborhood] was seen as a government-funded ghetto."

Although the first wave of revitalization attempts began in the 1990s, mostly with short-lived bars and clubs, the neighborhood didn't see any meaningful entrepreneurialism until the 21st century. And the new century brought its own set of issues.

As Margo Warminski, preservation director at the Cincinnati Preservation Association (CPA) says, "By the 2000s, Over-the-Rhine had lost so many people that it was literally full of vacant, empty, and decaying buildings. There were thousands of them. You can check the census data and it's really kind of shocking. [The population] was down to like 5,000 people some years ago."

Musicians Move In

All told, even Over-the-Rhine's vibrant history and astounding architecture couldn't save it from urban blight. Even as late as 2009, Cincinnati's local Fox News station cited an AOL finance website that claimed Over-the-Rhine was the most dangerous neighborhood in America, followed by neighborhoods in Chicago, Miami, Jacksonville, and Baltimore.

But this reputation for violence, desecration, and dilapidation is what enabled musicians and artists like Over the Rhine to live there for so cheap in the 1990s. While Detweiler counts himself lucky for not experiencing any violence firsthand, he does recall volatile acts in the area. "There were people that were robbed or even killed," he says. "There was a musician who was killed just a few blocks north of where I lived. He was a bass player and I was playing bass in the band at the time, so this news story went out that there was a bass player killed in Over-the-Rhine. We were on tour and it was pre-internet and people were wondering if that was me."

Today, however, general safety isn't the primary concern along the major streets of Over-the-Rhine. The past decade especially has seen some of the most extreme and effective change, as the HUD contracts finally reached their up-to-40-year limits back in 2010. And with such magnificent architecture remaining, not-for-profits like the CPA and the Cincinnati Center City Development Corporation (3CDC), as well as smaller, location-based volunteer organizations like the Society for the Preservation of Music Hall, have begun working to bring arts and culture back to Over-the-Rhine.

In fact, 3CDC spent about $48 million to renovate Washington Park, the six-acre mixed-use green space by Music Hall. After it was closed completely for almost 18 months starting in 2011, a ribbon-cutting reopening ceremony took place on July 6, 2012, and included a performance by the Over the Rhine.

"When I lived down there, it was basically a little wasteland where people go to shoot up and sleep on benches," says Detweiler. "But they did this glorious restoration of Washington Park and turned it into a stunningly beautiful green space with an amphitheater and lots and lots of trees and a dog park and small water park where kids can run around and play. When they finally got it renovated, they asked us to come down and play and do an inaugural performance/concert in that space. That was really a turning point. I think six or seven thousand people came out for that concert and just hung out in the park. That really felt like a stake in the ground like, 'This is not your father's Over-the-Rhine.' "

First Responders

These days, Over-the-Rhine is the hip part of Cincinnati. Lines for dinner reservations overflow from restaurant foyers into sidewalks lining Vine Street or Main Street. The new craft breweries like Rhinegeist (even on the less-developed north side of the neighborhood) draw their own kind of tourists and regulars. Custom soy candle shops sit next to stores with customized regional sportswear and carefully

Linford Detweiler and Karin Bergquist (Over The Rhine).

curated boutiques. In less than 10 years, the neighborhood went from mentions alongside Compton and parts of the South Side of Chicago to being compared to the trendier parts of Brooklyn and even Portland, Oregon.

While Over the Rhine initially informed audiences around the world about this tiny Cincinnati neighborhood they used to call home just with their name, other musical entrepreneurs have helped turn the historical district into a thriving community with a tight-knit arts scene. In particular, the team at MOTR Pub — an acronym for Music in Over-the-Rhine — has led the way.

MOTR co-owners Dan McCabe, Chris Schadler, and Chris Varias opened the 150-capacity brewpub in 2010, renovating a building from 1878 that had been boarded up and foreclosed for the previous five years. Four years later, they acquired the old Woodward Theater across the street (another historical property, this one from 1913). They gutted the old movie house and transformed it into a larger, 600-capacity venue.

On a recent afternoon, McCabe sits at the bar at the Woodward with a beer in hand and a MacBook open. He has just finished changing one of the windows on the second floor of the old venue because these are the things you do when you run

a burgeoning venue with a very small team. Emails from no fewer than three accounts stare back at him from the screen, but he looks away, preferring to make eye contact and talk about his city and its venues.

Having grown up in southern Ohio, McCabe's dedication to the area runs deep. He has worked in music for 30 years and continues to book bands for both MOTR and Woodward Theater. McCabe's first musical success came in the form of his first venue, Sudsy Malone's Rock 'n Roll Laundry & Bar near the University of Cincinnati (a haunt Detweiler fondly remembers playing and attending), which closed in 2005. Now he helps bring local and national music to Over-the-Rhine. MOTR hosts free shows seven nights a week, with food and drink sales offsetting each band's flat fee. And the club has seen growth in each of its six years in business.

It didn't start off easy, though. McCabe remembers the days when he and Schadler had to rely heavily on their old musical connections to help lure people to Over-the-Rhine. "We were kind of pioneering when we opened [MOTR] six years ago," he says. "A lot of stuff was just south of us and we were pretty far north. We were kind of dangling in the wind there when we first opened."

He pauses to consider how the neighborhood has been revitalized, then adds, "The people who like music, musicians, artists ... [those] are the urban pioneers. Those are the first responders."

Planning and Playing

One of the new local bands that has benefitted from MOTR and the Woodward Theater's existence is Dawg Yawp. The duo, comprised of Tyler Randall on sitar and Rob Keenan on guitar, released its self-titled debut album last October. A strange combination of American blues and folk, English psychedelic, and traditional Indian sounds, Dawg Yawp most engagingly infuses their roots influences into songs like their take on the traditional tune "East Virginia Blues" and others like "Dawg" that have repetitive guitar lines evocative of the Hill Country blues.

"We got our start playing all over the area," Randall says over email, "from the Southgate House in Newport, Kentucky, to the Crow's Nest on the west side of [Cincinnati]. Those two places are where we encountered the most American roots music, such as the Tillers, and we were greatly inspired."

As Dawg Yawp continued to hone

"No good city and no good city neighborhood is just all poor or all black or all white or all rich. A good neighborhood is supposed to be a mix of classes and a mix of everything."

Chris Schadler (MOTR Pub)

their sound and grow their local audience, Randall and Keenan moved to the similarly nascent Northside. But with support from McCabe and Schadler, Over-the-Rhine became a surrogate home for the band, too. MOTR even hosted the group's album release party last October.

MOTR/Woodward Theater co-owner Schadler does a lot of thinking about the future of music in Over-the-Rhine. A native of the area, he has "been booking shows and playing in bands and in the music scene for a very long time — we'll just leave it at that!" he says with a laugh. Additionally, Schadler earned his master's degree in urban planning at the University of Cincinnati's Design, Architecture, Art, and Planning program, using his thesis to assess the relationship between music and urban development. "The two worlds collided," he says. "Being a rock and roll promoter and then having a planning degree, you start seeing connections and the way the two kind of fit together."

In Over-the-Rhine, Schadler has seen positive developments so far, though he's seen it go another way elsewhere in Cincinnati, which makes him cautious. Eleven years ago, for example, he began the Northside Rock 'N Roll Carnival. After the second edition, Schadler recalls, he went into a local bar and talked with the bartender about the event. The couple

sitting next him told him that they ended up buying a house in the neighborhood because they had such a great time at the festival.

"There are many, many people who want to be in a place that is exciting and there's fun stuff going on and you can have spontaneous experiences," Schadler says. Then he follows with a story about one of the hillside neighborhoods that became known for its music community years ago. When the cost of rent went up for residents and businesses, none of the people who helped create the scene could afford to live there anymore, leaving the area homogenous and dull.

"Now with all the renaissance going on, the big question, of course, is [how] gentrification [will play out]," he says. "No good city and no good city neighborhood is just all poor or all black or all white or all rich. A good neighborhood is supposed to be a mix of classes and a mix of everything."

As Schadler's two venues continue to prosper alongside the other restaurants, bars, shops, condos, and more in Over-the-Rhine, he fears that the rapid redevelopment and market growth will stunt the area's inclusivity and diversity. "To keep it diverse should be [the city's] number-one priority, because the market is responding and people are moving in, and so now they need to make sure it's a

robust area," he cautions. "Without getting too heady about it, you've got to try to ensure ways to have a population that's diverse — both racially and economically."

For the time being, though, Over-the-Rhine is thriving in a way that seemed incomprehensible less than a decade ago. It's not yet perfect nor fully renovated, but cities are fluid entities that never cease to evolve.

From the classical and choral performances that will return to their rightful home at the Music Hall when renovations conclude this fall, to the venues like MOTR and the Woodward Theater, to roots musicians like Over the Rhine, Katie Lauer, the Tillers, and Dawg Yawp, music is an undeniable force helping bring people back to a neighborhood that was once forsaken.

One recent day, on the steps outside Holtman's Donuts, a popular bakery on Vine Street, a middle-aged father wearing a baseball cap held the door as his son ambled inside. Upon recognizing neighborhood advocate Jim Tarbell standing there, he turned around and asked cheerfully, "Mr. Tarbell, is this neighborhood almost the way you envisioned it yet?"

Dressed in his overcoat with a sticker that proclaimed, "I made a difference and so can you. VOTE," Tarbell replied with a grin: "It's getting there." ■

THE **SADDLE CREEK** SOUND

In some ways, Conor Oberst put Nebraska on the map

By Lee Zimmerman

"I N A WORLD OF PAPER *tigers and imaginary friends It's a shame I can't be bothered to pretend When I'm standing on the outside looking in."*
— Conor Oberst,
"Standing on the Outside Looking In"

Whether Conor Oberst had his hometown of Omaha, Nebraska, in mind when he wrote that song is a matter of conjecture. Still, there's no doubt that the lyrics reflect a certain sensibility that comes with living in the middle of America, far from the bustling, trend-setting capitals of culture.

Geographically, Omaha is about as close to the middle of America as one can get. Founded in 1854 on the banks of the Missouri River, it feels as if it's miles from anything else that resembles a metropolis. Historically, the city's claims to fame include being an important railway junction for the transportation of goods across the country in the 19th century and, more recently, being the headquarters for Fortune 500 companies like Mutual of Omaha and Berkshire Hathaway.

Musically, Omaha has a long, deep cultural history, as celebrated by its Black Music Hall of Fame. Also of interest, it carries an unexpected connection to the sounds of Scotland, represented these days by a resident ensemble known as

the Strathdon Caledonia Pipe Band. In fact, Omaha's musical legacy stretches all the way back to 1893, when composer Antonín Dvořák visited the city and came away so impressed and inspired that he wrote his New World Symphony based on those impressions.

But for the better part of the 20th century, Omaha missed out on making a name for itself. Not surprisingly then, when Omaha native Conor Oberst started playing guitar with his friends at the age of 12, he did so mostly just to occupy his idle time.

"There really wasn't much of a scene back then," Oberst recalls. "I started playing music when I was 12, 13 years old, and it was mainly me and my friends getting together to just fool around. We weren't thinking it would be anything serious. I guess you could say we were playing mostly punk music at the time, some grunge as well. This was the early '90s, after all. There wasn't a lot to do, and playing music was kind of a cure for all the boredom. Plus, there were a lot of good basements where we could go to practice."

Soon, Oberst started writing songs, and he became a prolific songwriter. The earliest tunes he committed to tape in his parents' basement found their way to his first self-released cassettes, the beginnings of what would eventually become an expansive music catalog.

"My parents were real supportive," he says. "I mean, they were willing to put this 15-year-old kid in a van to go out on tour. What does that say?

"When things started kicking in, in 2004, 2005, it got pretty overwhelming," he adds. "But mostly I was like any other kid growing up. I did a lot of stupid stuff, did the usual drugs and things like that. Most kids have a hard time adjusting when they're growing up anyway. ... I did my best to get good grades in school so that I could show my folks that I wasn't slacking off because of the music."

Oberst spent three semesters at the University of Nebraska, but eventually dropped out, convinced that he was far more suited to a career in music. Once again, his parents supported his decision. "I went to my parents and said, 'Hey, it looks like this music thing is taking off and I'd like to pursue it,'" he remembers. "They were fine with that. They said, 'If that's what you want to do, then go out and do it.'"

In time, Oberst's musical ventures expanded even further, and he became an integral member of a number of daring, imaginative bands — The Faint, Commander Venus, Park Ave., the Magnetas, Desaparecidos, the Mystic Valley Band, Monsters of Folk, and, of course, Bright Eyes, the moniker he used early on for his solo efforts. Some of those projects barely lasted; others made a

Looking west down Leavenworth Street in Omaha.

formidable impression far beyond his Nebraska home, gaining national prominence before Oberst was out of his 20s.

And yet, he says, "there was no real financial success to speak of. It's only been in the last ten years ... that it became apparent things were really happening and the career was taking off. But really, the three of us — me, Mike [Mogis], and Andy [LeMaster] — never really thought about it. We never make albums with the critics in mind. We don't really worry about meeting any sort of expectations or preconceptions from our fans. We don't make music for the sake of the reviews. We're just trying to please ourselves and make music we like."

Over the course of approximately 25 years, Oberst and his various outfits have released numerous albums, earning all kinds of accolades in the process. He's proven himself to be a wunderkind of sorts, certainly one of the youngest rock stars on record given the fact that he was making music as early as his mid-teens. By the time he reached his early 20s, he had an international following.

LeMaster — a singer-songwriter and producer who worked on several of the early Bright Eyes albums and still works with Oberst — credits his friend's success to his open-mindedness and discriminating taste. "[Conor has a] strong sense of what does or doesn't work for a song," he says. "He's always willing to try some new approach, and he often embraces and incorporates new suggestions, but he's also very clear on whether or not a particular approach is appropriate. He's great about not wasting too much time going down any one particular rabbit hole."

Oberst takes that comment a step further. "I feel [a] sense of responsibility," he says. "It make[s] me feel a little vulnerable. ... But these days, it's pretty much Mike and Andy and me that are involved with everything. So I'm not totally on my own. Mike lives close by, so we're always able to run down to the studio we both share and record when we like."

The Saddle Creek Start-Up

Oberst has become somewhat the face of the Omaha music scene, in part because he did more than merely claim it as his home turf. Along with his brother Justin and his long-time musical collaborator Mike Mogis, he started a record label and based it in his hometown. He originally called the label Lumberjack Records but eventually renamed it Saddle Creek, after a street that cuts through Omaha's midtown.

Initially the home for Bright Eyes, The Faint, and other assorted local outfits, Saddle Creek Records eventually opened its doors to bands from other areas of the country, including indie rockers like Sorry About Dresden, Rilo Kiley, Georgie James, Two Gallants, and Tokyo Police Club.

"At first, it was pretty much the means of releasing my early project, those first cassettes I did," Oberst explains. "It was very homegrown and very rudimentary at that point. And then it took off very slowly. Eventually, we started signing other artists. Once it started taking off, it was pretty exciting. ... But eventually it started becoming your typical corporate record company, following the usual corporate business models."

Oberst has since left the label,

branching out with a sister label called Team Love before signing with Nonesuch Records. Even so, he maintains that indie ethos and Saddle Creek remains the region's best-known record label, one that epitomizes the ideals that so many Midwest musicians represent.

"I feel artists from the Midwest have a certain sincerity and lack of pretense," says Mogis. "In Conor's case, I feel it's made his writing [and] performances — and our recording style — more honest and raw. We think it's easier for people to connect to a song the more genuine and real it feels. I think people from the Midwest generally don't like things too polished or slick, because it seems insincere or something."

LeMaster sees this definitive sound — which has come to be called the Saddle Creek Sound — as the result of some good old-fashioned Midwestern prag-matism. "Several of my Midwestern artist friends, including Conor," he says, "have an inherent pragmatic business acumen, so I kind of consider that a Midwestern sensibility — an intuitive practical sense of what works and what's appropriate for the presentation of his art."

Despite his allegiance to that Midwest sensibility, Oberst spent a decade living in New York City — probably more for the sake of convenience than to escape any sense of geographic isolation. "I never really thought about [how isolated Nebraska is]," he muses. "At least not until we started touring. That's when we realized that we'd have to be in a van for eight hours before we could get anywhere."

Though he found some benefits to living in New York, eventually he and his wife, Corina Escamilla Figueroa, returned to Omaha, eager to embrace it as home. The lyrics from his song "NYC - Gone, Gone" offer some insight into his sentiments at the time of his departure.

Gone, gone from New York City
Where you gonna go
with a head that empty?
Gone, gone from New York City
Where you gonna go
with a heart that gone?

"A lot of the people we knew there eventually moved away," he explains. "And the ones that stayed moved to Brooklyn and Queens. I like New York, but it's very hectic. Omaha is a lot more laid back. I like

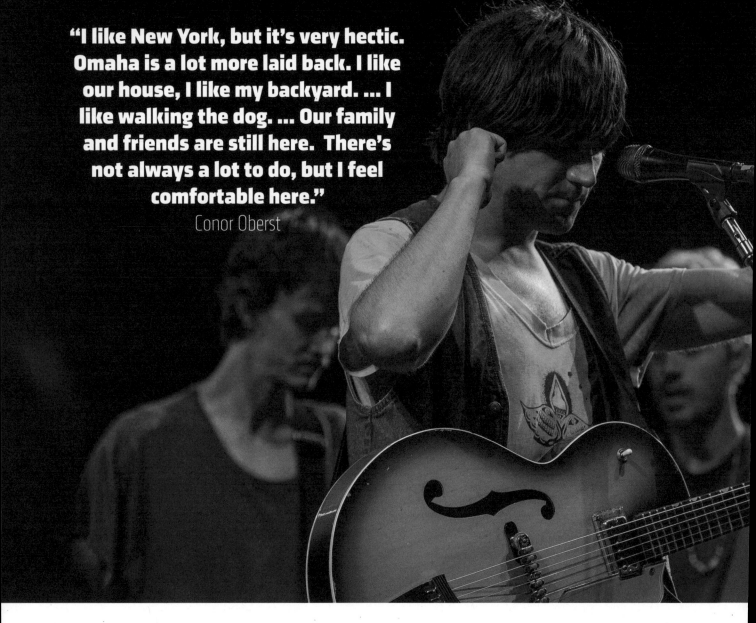

> "I like New York, but it's very hectic. Omaha is a lot more laid back. I like our house, I like my backyard. ... I like walking the dog. ... Our family and friends are still here. There's not always a lot to do, but I feel comfortable here."
>
> Conor Oberst

our house, I like my backyard. ... I like walking the dog. We've thought about different places where we could live, but with the list of cities we've come up with so far, nothing really jumps out at us. We might get another place somewhere else at some point, but I think we'll always keep the house we have here. Our family and friends are still here. There's not always a lot to do, but I feel comfortable here."

Reflections and Ruminations

Indeed, Oberst's hometown directly impacted the creation of his 2016 album, appropriately called *Ruminations*. He wrote the whole thing while stuck at home due to some typically tempestuous winter weather.

"It was really cold outside," he says.

"The snow was falling and most of the time I was alone late at night when my wife was asleep. So I'd retreat to a room by myself and write. When I brought the demos to my record label, my point person liked what he heard. I had planned to add some arrangements and embellishment, but he told me that they wanted to release it as it was. That was pretty astute. It's obviously sparse, but that's the way they wanted it, and that's how it turned out. It's a solo record in every sense of the word."

Ruminations is not only Oberst's most personal recording to date, but also his most spare. His first actual solo recording in 20 years, it's filled with melancholy musings, sad story-songs that bring reflection and remorse to the fore. With only piano, acoustic guitar, and harmonica

as accompaniment, Oberst took the time and space to ponder life through the lens of introversion and solitude.

At times the sentiments in these songs feel almost as isolated as Omaha itself, but like those railways of the Midwest, the connection runs not only through the heartland but through the hearts of its listeners as well.

At the same time, several of these songs are unceasingly downcast. In "Next of Kin," he sings:

Saw a crash on the interstate
It left a feeling I could not shake
Just a name in a database
That must be notified.

Then there's this from "Gossamer Thin":

*Rings round his eyes,
tracks down his arm
His fans are confused
and his friends are alarmed.*

Oberst grabs your heart with a fist when he lands on the line, "You all loved him once," which carries equal parts nostalgia and blame.

"Conor's unwavering devotion to the art of lyric writing is, and has always been, as strong as I've ever seen in an artist," Mogis says. "His bar is just higher than anyone else I've ever worked with. Keeping true to that high standard and discipline while continuously producing quality songs, year after year, album after album, well, that is pretty special. ... Plus, the fact that he has never really given a fuck about what anyone thinks has been

kind of refreshing."

LeMaster concurs. "I don't know of another contemporary lyricist in his category," he says. "His gift of poetry and command of language is so powerful. It's like a physical force. He can weave a cohesive theme through vivid flashes of patchwork imagery and make it seem effortless. And like a great artist should, he often challenges comfort zones, both in his writing and live performances. Part of his unique gift is inspiring his audience to question what they think they know."

For all the solitude and rumination the new album shares, Oberst is anything but isolated nowadays. In fact, the new disc — and his participation in a tribute to Emmylou Harris — has had him busy on the road, in the publicity machine of new albums and late night TV show tapings. But

when he was finally available to talk for this story, he was as cordial, cooperative, and expressive as his collaborators noted, especially when the conversation shifted to his Midwest origins and the influence Omaha had on him early on.

He also sees what the city has become, how its growth has, at least in part, resulted from his success in sharing Omaha's sound with the world. And he's willing to concede that he's become something of a hometown hero. "Maybe I am," he says. "People are very nice and they've always been very supportive."

Naturally, with that success comes certain perks. Among them: "I don't have to wait in line at restaurants," he beams, before adding that, like so many people in so many small towns, "I know most of the restaurant owners." ■

Houses
in the
Fields

Development in the heartland has long been a
ripe theme for songwriting, from Chrissie Hynde's
"My City Was Gone" to John Gorka's "Houses in the
Fields." This theme has drawn ever more attention
in recent years, in light of oil pipelines and wind
farms and other changes to the landscape. So we
checked with visual artist and Iowa native Justin
Amable for some images that capture what Gorka's
song so beautifully talks about:

Two more farms were broken by the drought
First the Wagners now the Fullers are pulling out
Developers pay better than the corn
But this was not the place where they were born
They're growing houses in the fields ...

— Kim Ruehl
Images by Justin Amable

NATIVE ON THE MIC

On reservations and in cities, America's first people wield the power of hip-hop

by Corbie Hill

Frank Waln

> "People call me an activist, and I just say I am indigenous. I am Lakota. Our worldview is older than the word 'activist.' I'm just making music about my life. Would you call a white country music artist['s work] 'identity music'? They're just making music about their life."
>
> Frank Waln

FROM THE AIRPORT IN Bismarck, North Dakota, it's about an hour and a half to the small town of Solen, and then another 10 or 15 minutes to the Dakota Access Pipeline protest camp at Standing Rock. In late October 2016, Tanaya Winder made her second trip to the small town as part of a poetry-in-schools program, to work with the students of Solen High, which has a total student population of less than 100.

Winder — a poet and spoken-word artist who manages Native hip-hop artists Frank Waln, Tall Paul, Mic Jordan, and Def-I — joined her sister in Solen and spent all of that Monday leading workshops. After school, one of the teachers took them to the camp. It was cold, Winder recalls, and there were a lot of tents set up. Flagpoles lined the road, each one for a tribe or other supporter of the anti-pipeline movement. People were singing and dancing and holding signs by the road. There were babies and elders and people of all ages, some on horseback — it was beautiful, she says.

Sacred Stone Camp was established early in 2016 with the goal of stopping construction on a section of the Dakota Access Pipeline that would cross the Missouri River. The pipeline is a thousand-mile underground oil line connecting North Dakota to a small southern Illinois town. Members of the Standing Rock Sioux tribe were concerned about its impact on sacred sites and its potential to pollute the river, which runs through a number of cities downstream. Despite law enforcement meeting the water protectors with attack dogs, rubber bullets, and water cannons in subfreezing North Dakota winter weather, the camp grew in size and crept into the national dialogue, largely via social media. In December 2016, the Army Corps of Engineers denied the easement that would have allowed the pipeline to cross the Missouri River. As of press time, the water protectors were celebrating the decision.

A month before Winder arrived there, indigenous rapper Drezus spent close to two weeks in the Standing Rock camps, and he wants to go back. Beyond uplifting, he says, it was a life-changing experience. "It was beautiful, man," he says. "Especially the gatherings they'd have on the weekends. Saturday nights, having all the tribes from all the country share their songs — dancing, laughing, basically partying without drugs and alcohol.

"We planted trees in the way of the

pipeline," he adds with pride. "Obviously they came and tore the shit out the same day. [But] it was a really small victory, you know? We're definitely getting the word out."

Drezus, who lives 800 miles from Standing Rock, in Calgary, Alberta, has two platforms: he can show up in person to speak out with his people, and he can make music. Appropriately, he's written a slew of pro-Standing Rock songs. One, "Long Live the People," is intentionally upbeat and uplifting. Rather than delve into the depressing details of the #NoDAPL protest — the arrests, the militarized police, the paucity of media coverage, the likelihood that the pipeline's completion is inevitable — Drezus celebrates the powerful indigenous spirit.

> *War cry for all the times*
> *I ain't get a chance*
> *Cops want me to act up,*
> *I got bigger plans*
> *I'm a Native boy*
> *Let me do this for my Natives, bruh.*

As is true across all protest song traditions, Drezus believes that people who might not otherwise be open to the message might simply like how the song sounds at first. And once they like the sound of it, he hopes they'll open their ears to what he's saying. The overarching message for this Native rapper is the same one his peers echo: how vital it is to tell the true stories about the lives of Native people.

Culture Shock

When Frank Waln moved from rural South Dakota to Chicago for college, he experienced severe culture shock. He'd grown up on a ranch in a tiny plains community and had never seen a skyscraper before. Now he was living in a

Tanaya Winder

dorm room downtown. The city excited him — it still does — but four years ago everything was new.

One day during his first week, he recalls, he was riding the elevator in his building when the girl beside him turned and said, "You have really pretty hair. What are you?"

"Thank you," Waln told her. "I'm Lakota." Her reply: a blank look. "I'm Native American," he clarified.

"You guys are still alive?" she asked, incredulous.

"She thought we were extinct," Waln recalls. It was his first exposure to that level of ignorance, and he was shaken. After all, here was a college-educated person who had no idea America's indigenous people still existed. She'd been getting the wrong story. Wherever this woman had been getting her information, Waln knew, it wasn't from a Native source.

This short conversation set his thoughts in motion: he knew he had to do something to share true stories about his people. This young Lakota, raised on the Rosebud Reservation in the small community of He Dog, decided he would use hip-hop to do just that.

He's not alone: rap is a force in indigenous music in both the US and Canada. Among its budding stars are Waln, who splits his time between Chicago and the Rosebud Reservation, and Tall Paul, whose south Minneapolis upbringing intersects with his desire to connect with his Native heritage. In Calgary, Drezus spits raw, hard-edged rhymes. Billings, Montana-based Supaman raps and dances in a Fancy Dance costume — the kind of extravagant, headdress-and-feathers outfit that's more common at powwows. And in Seattle, one of Native hip-hop's progenitors, Litefoot, works tirelessly to help his people. Twenty-five years into his career as a rapper, actor, entrepreneur, and motivational speaker, Litefoot has made it his life's work to help his fellow indigenous Americans.

Tall Paul

A lot of these artists' rhymes sound like protest music. Indeed, several of them note that hip-hop is the contemporary music of the oppressed, the music of social change. More accurately, these rappers are telling true stories about Native life in a format that's equally accessible for the listener and the creator.

"People call me an activist, and I just say I am indigenous," Waln says. "I am Lakota. Our worldview is older than the word 'activist.'"

Waln adds that, when he writes a song, he's simply writing about his life. He knows other people may see it as protest or political music, but that's because Native American lives are implicitly, inextricably political. They have been affected by the US government since the Europeans colonized North America, and thus US laws and politics impact him whether he wants them to or not, whether he realizes it or not.

Even the premise of Native American music being about Native identity casts indigenous people as an other.

"I'm just making music about my life," he says. "Would you call a white country music artist['s work] 'identity music?' They're just making music about their life."

Waln's life began in He Dog, a reservation community of maybe 30 households in the southern quadrant of South Dakota. In the entire Rosebud Reservation, a swath of land about the size of Rhode Island, there is one stoplight. The population of its capital, the unincorporated town of Rosebud, hovered just below 1,600 as of the 2010 census. As a child, Waln lived out in the country, surrounded by family. There were plenty of kids in He Dog, and they were mostly his cousins and siblings.

"It was a ranch run by Native women

> "A lot of people are under the assumption that we don't make music. A lot of people don't know about Native people, period."
>
> Drezus

in one of the poorest places in the country," Waln explains. "We all had to work and we all had to help each other, and help the family out."

Waln's family had been in He Dog since his mom was in high school; farther back, he can trace family history back to his great-great-great grandparents. He doesn't know the older stories, he says — not yet, anyway. And while there are certainly other artistic people in his family, Waln is the only one to have left home to pursue it. "I come from a rodeo family," he explains. "Most of my cousins, they rodeo. I'm kind of the odd one out."

Waln's mom, who raised him, enabled his artistry. Growing up, there was music playing in the house: country acts like George Strait, Garth Brooks, and Dwight Yoakam, and classic rockers like Fleetwood Mac and Creedence Clearwater Revival. When he was 7, Waln's elementary school teacher noticed he gravitated toward the piano. Waln would sit there, dedicated, and try to figure out the instrument. When the teacher told his mom, she got him piano lessons from an older woman in the community. As Waln grew, he diversified: he began to write poetry, to play drums in the pep band, and to produce music, though it took him a while to gain the confidence to share his creations.

"I was maybe 12 and I heard a song by Nas," he says. The influential New York rapper's track "One Mic" still moves him. "I like the progression. When he starts off almost whispering, by the end he's screaming. The music tells a story. He's telling a very specific story, speaking to his people.

"When I heard that song, I thought, 'I

want to be a hip-hop artist,'" he continues. "And I'm going to do whatever it takes to make that happen."

A Universal Language

To Tall Paul, hip-hop is more than just a music genre. It crosses demographic lines, connecting people of all kinds of backgrounds: white people, black people, suburban people and those in the inner city, and so many others. It's a huge platform, he explains, and it can be very powerful because it reaches so many people.

"I don't know if there's another music genre that reaches as diverse a background of fans. It crosses age groups, from kids up to adults," says Tall Paul (who is six-foot-three and who was born Paul Wenell Jr.). "More personally, it gives me a voice to inspire and motivate others."

Like Waln, Tall Paul is telling his own story. He frequently hears from listeners who find themselves in his lyrics and experience a very real human connection. Though he doesn't always think about how to make that connection when he's writing — he says his objective is usually to write for the sake of writing — he is moved when people reach out for those connections, telling him, "I grew up in an inner city," or "I'm light-skinned, so a lot of people don't see me as being Native."

Tall Paul is Ojibwe, and was raised in Minneapolis. For his first seven years, his home life was toxic. On the outside, it likely seemed fine, he says. But his stepfather was abusive and his mom eventually moved herself and the kids into Tall Paul's grandmother's house. He was midway through elementary school

before he met his biological father.

Like Waln, he was surrounded by family, though he doesn't speak as fondly of his childhood as his Lakota friend does. His grandmother's house was always packed with aunts, uncles, cousins, and siblings — always drinking, always partying. "Growing up in that environment," he says, "you start thinking some abnormal things are normal."

From a young age, Tall Paul wanted to have a career; he wanted to grow up to be a good dad and husband. As a teenager, though, he remembers wanting to fit in with the older crowd. He started getting interested in girls, but all the girls he was around were partiers, too. He just didn't see any young people doing positive things with their time. "One day, one of my cousins was like, 'Hey, Paul. Hit this joint,'" he remembers. "And that's it."

He'd been active in sports, but that went out the window. For the next few years, he was up to no good: drinking, smoking, partying, and getting in trouble with the law. Today, Paul is sober, and he has been for years. It was hip-hop, he says, that saved him.

Hustle or Life

Drezus also knows how hard it is to quit. Drugs provided an escape, but there was money in them, too. "I still have urges to do that," he confesses; sometimes he misses the hustle. "Especially with this rap shit. It doesn't pay all the time. Some days I want to be like, 'Fuck this, I want to get back on it.'"

The multiple award-winning Cree-Ojibwe rapper was born Jeremiah

Manitopyes in Saskatoon, Canada. Now he calls Calgary home. When he picks up the phone, though, he's in Fairbanks, Alaska, for a rare gig in that US state. It's all a matter of spreading the word, he says practically.

"A lot of people are under the assumption that we don't make music," he says. "A lot of people don't know about Native people, period."

As a child, Drezus never fit in. Saskatoon had a large Native population and a lot of problems; Calgary was more white-collar and multicultural, he says, but he was perpetually on the outside. He was raised by his mom — a hard-working woman whom he admired. But while she was at work during the day, he was on his own.

He did well in school, strengthening his intellect and writing poetry. But then he found drugs and alcohol young, and he remembers looking up to gang members he saw in the city. They'd be out barking orders to their younger subordinates and getting drunk and high. Their particular kind of power was attractive to him at the time, and among other things that changed for him, his taste in music shifted from Run-DMC, which opened his mind to the existence and power of hip-hop, toward subversive acts like Ice-T and NWA. Their violent lyrics in particular drew him in.

"There was times when I wouldn't want to be around anybody, man," he says. "I didn't fit in — I was the fat little Native kid with buckteeth and shit. I didn't fit in with nobody. The only place I did feel comfortable was sitting in the room, listening to hip-hop and ... smoking weed, drinking, doing whatever I did."

Thus, drugs and alcohol dominated his life for years. He had a son when he was just 18 (he also has a younger son who lives in New Mexico), but fatherhood alone wasn't enough to wake him up. It wasn't until 2012, when he was in a rehab program in Winnipeg as part of his sentence for a drug charge, that Drezus

began to turn his life around. His older son, whom he hadn't lived with in nearly a decade, called and asked, "When are you coming home, Dad?"

Drezus says that call placed a very real choice in front of him: hustle or life. The next week, he packed up and went back to Calgary. "Basically, I just started over," he says. "I was just like a baby. Seriously — relearning how to live legally, that was a major wake-up call."

The Next Generation

Just as Drezus's son helped pull him back to sobriety, so too did Tall Paul's. Tall Paul quit drinking in late 2008, just as he entered his 20s. He'd spent a weekend in prison and was court-ordered to stay sober, but it was his interest in being a good father to his six-month-old son that made the change stick.

Though many parents can relate to the urge to clean up their lives in order to live well for their children, the connection between artists and children is a deep tradition in Native communities. Many Native rappers work with Native youth, becoming role models, examples of people who both own their heritage and follow their dreams. A lot of young indigenous people, says Winder, really need to see this. A lot of them live in poverty or have responsibilities to take care of their grandparents or siblings. These children see their parents living paycheck to paycheck, and they're always in crisis mode. They don't get the privilege of long-term thinking.

"Our Native youth are dying," says Supaman, whose given name is Christian Parrish Takes the Gun. "They're committing suicide. They're on drugs and alcohol."

He knows what he's talking about. The Montana-based rapper works on suicide prevention with a group called Sources of Strength, blending powwow culture and hip-hop into something youth can grab onto and make their own. Like Tall Paul and Drezus, Supaman is sober these days.

Born and raised Apsáalooke — more commonly known as Crow, thanks to a long-ago mistranslation, he notes — Supaman grew up doing his tribe's dances. Though Fancy Dancing wasn't part of his own tradition, he saw Fancy Dancers at powwows when he was in elementary school and wanted to try that style: it was fast and energetic, and it looked like fun. His mother initially told him no, that he was Apsáalooke from Montana. But he persisted, driven by the fact that powwows aren't ceremonial events specific to any one culture, but rather social celebrations. The Men's Fancy, he argued, was becoming as universal as the powwows themselves. Eventually his mother relented and allowed him to try Fancy Dancing, and he's been doing it ever since.

"It's a contemporary style. There is no spiritual significance to it," Supaman explains. "It was made for the show, for the people who are watching the dance. There's a lot of dancers doing flips and splits and a couple of b-boy moves. I even did the Worm a couple of times while I was dancing."

When Supaman first started rapping, he kept his worlds of music and dance separate: he would wear his elaborate costume when he danced and then switch to something more casual when he rapped. Then, at one powwow dancing exhibition in Bozeman, that wall came down. He'd been asked to dance and rap at the same event. When he left the stage to change into his rap clothes, he was told there was no time. There was not another speaker, and the crowd was waiting. He returned to the stage in his Fancy Dance outfit and got on the mic.

After the show, one of the elders approached Supaman. "Oh, man — he's going to scold [me]," the rapper thought, but instead the elder took off his hat and shook Supaman's hand.

"That was pretty damn powerful. That was pretty damn cool what you did up there," he remembers the elder telling him. "You guys showed the youth there

Supaman

that you embrace who you are as a Native and it's good to dance. You express that you're proud of your culture. At the same time, you spoke the language of the youth, which is rap music, and you had some good messages in your music. ... Keep doing that."

Easy Access, Hard Issues

This ability to bridge generations is hip-hop's power, Winder contends. Growing up on the Southern Ute Reservation in Colorado, she'd always gravitated toward the music. She could relate to the artists and to hip-hop's overall culture. When she went to Stanford for her undergrad degree, however, she started listening to a lot of Bay Area hip-hop and took a class on social protest drama and the politics of hip-hop. She studied Augusto Boal's *Theatre of the Oppressed* and began to understand the background and social justice elements of hip-hop.

For starters, she learned that rap can thrive anywhere — it's poetry, really, and doesn't always need a backing track or even a mic to be performed. If there's an issue to be discussed or if awareness needs to be raised, Winder contends, why not take it directly to the people?

"I loved the idea of meeting people where they're at," she says. "People don't always have access to learn about what's going on, particularly now with all the stuff with the Dakota Access Pipeline."

If it's accessible to listeners of all backgrounds, it's also incredibly accessible on the artist side. That's one thing that initially drew Seattle-based actor, rapper, and entrepreneur Litefoot in.

Born Gary Paul Davis in Oklahoma, Litefoot is perhaps best known to audiences on the coasts for his roles in films like *The Indian in the Cupboard* or *Mortal Kombat Annihilation*. These days, he is dedicated to giving voice to Native communities, and his entrée to entertainment was the accessibility of

hip-hop. It was a different creative space, he explains. If you didn't have access to musical instruments or know how to play one, you could still turn your thoughts into lyrics. Then you could use turntables and technology to create the music. Hip-hop eliminates the barriers for people who lack privilege or resources — kids from the projects or reservations, say — and provides them with a platform for self-expression.

"It was an opportunity to talk about things no one else was talking about. I could have a voice in that," Litefoot says. "Who's going to tell my story better than me? That really was exciting to me."

If hip-hop is universal and accessible, it's also born of social struggle. It was built for protest, Litefoot explains, and has long been the vehicle for songs about police brutality, black power, and social inequality. Listen to Tupac Shakur's "Brenda's Got a Baby," Litefoot suggests, citing the 1991 classic as a prime example.

Litefoot

"We always have to remember [that] our words and what we speak into this earth [are] medicine. And you have to be careful with your medicine, man, especially when you know that's your gift and your power."

Litefoot

As he works on his upcoming album, his first since 2008, Litefoot — whom Tall Paul and others credit as an early inspiration — keeps in mind that hip-hop was built to be revolutionary music. Now is a volatile time, he says, and he wants to be honest and real. He can't just talk about problems; the songs have to offer solutions as well. "Being Native," he says, "we always have to remember [that] our words and what we speak into this earth [are] medicine," he says. "And you have to be careful with your medicine, man, especially when you know that's your gift and your power."

Tall Paul breaks that idea down for the layman, noting there's something insincere about writing a protest song simply because there's a hot-button topic. Issues tend to arise naturally anyway, and it's better not to force anything. Referring to his songs about standardized education and inequality in the US, he says, "part of it is a creative choice. I don't want to be one of many fish in the sea who have tackled this topic. I want to be true to myself and I don't want to make this [issue] a platform to get my name out there."

Tall Paul's ethics won't let him write about a serious or pressing topic until he has an honest inspiration. With the Dakota Access Pipeline, for instance, the honest inspiration came from a story a friend told him: There was a show in Fargo, and the rappers were explaining the anti-pipeline movement between songs. One woman in the crowd was just hearing about it for the first time, and she began drunkenly shouting the movement's #NoDAPL hashtag, but pronouncing it to rhyme with "apple." It became a bit of a joke, with others at the show shouting it too. They were making fun, but also recognizing the seriousness of the issue.

Then an image came to Tall Paul's mind. In both the Native art and the lore surrounding the pipeline protest, the pipeline is often represented as a black snake. The rapper — also a visual artist — pictured an elementary school illustration of an apple with a worm poking out of it, only instead of a worm, it was a black snake. And then the song "Bad DAPL" came to him.

While some songs come in the form of images such as that one, other times, all the rage — the historical trauma, as Waln and Supaman call it — that comes with understanding post-colonial indigenous history explodes in a single track. On Columbus Day, Waln released "7," a ferocious track that features elements of Winder's poem "Back to the Beginning." The song has been in Waln's set for years, but it felt right to put it out in 2016. As the intense track wraps up, he barks:

The system try to hold us down
You forced our cultures underground
But you ain't stopping no one now
We're stronger and we know it now.

Then the backing track ends, and for the song's last minute the only sounds are Waln sobbing and an elder speaking in his native tongue. ■

BIG SKY SPIRIT

Independent Montanans embrace the singer-songwriter

by Skip Anderson

HUNDREDS OF WHITE folding chairs dotted a Montana hillside during a late-summer sunset. Their formation unfurled in the shadow of the great Roosevelt Arch at the North Entrance to Yellowstone National Park. Around six thousand people attended the event: the National Park Service's centennial celebration. Barack Obama delivered his recorded well-wishes via a video on a large screen, and actor/Montana resident Bill Pullman, who emceed the evening, kept the banter light between remarks by bureaucrats and politicians that inched the evening toward its musical headliners. Famously independent in spirit, Montanans have limited patience for bureaucrats, but they are much more inclined to listen to a politician should he or she express a genuine appreciation of nature's splendor — a value virtually all Montanans hold dear. It was an all-American event at the front door of the world's very first national park, and its planners turned to American roots music luminaries Emmylou Harris and John Prine to headline the celebration.

While Montana's oldest musical tradition unquestionably belongs to Native American groups who first inhabited the region centuries before statehood, its contemporary landscape is dominated by singer-songwriters.

"The music scene here, both historically and currently, is Americana and roots music," says Mike "Bueno" Good, owner of Cactus Records in Bozeman. "There was a bluegrass phase in the early 2000s, right around the time *O Brother[, Where Art Thou?]* came out. That really hit home with a lot of people."

Montanans, in general, appreciate personal responsibility, and the one person-one guitar approach to earnest music-making seems to appeal to that sensibility.

"Montana's music scene has evolved naturally since I first came here in the 1970s," says Dave Goodwin, a producer and songwriter who relocated from Nashville to Montana in 2000. "You're inspired by the environment here. Artists can get back to a space where they really connect with people, and that's lost in other places."

Indoors and Outdoors

Montana is the fourth-largest state in the country in terms of landmass. To put that in perspective, the state is larger than the 18 smallest countries in Europe combined. That's including Belgium, Switzerland, The Netherlands, and Denmark. And you'd find no more success in unifying a patchwork of disparate, spread-out people and cultures than Montana and its rich musical portrait.

The state has no fewer than eight symphonies. KGLT in Bozeman, an NPR-aligned (but not formally affiliated) radio station that reaches audiences in the capital city of Helena as well as Livingston in Paradise Valley, is wonderfully format-free and features eclectic volunteer DJs who draw upon multiple genres at any given time. In Missoula, restored vaudeville house the Wilma and its sister venue, the Top Hat Lounge, bring in heavy hitters such as Sturgill Simpson and Josh Ritter. In the winters, big-name artists regularly perform at invitation-only house concerts for high-rollers in the

ski-resort town of Big Sky, while local cover bands in dance halls throughout the state carefully choose when to mix in an original song or two.

Winters here are long, and temperatures will inevitably dip to minus 20 degrees or colder even in the southernmost part of the state. But when the snow thaws, Montana's music scene heads outdoors.

Hamilton, Montana, offers the Hard Times Bluegrass Festival, and last year the Mavericks and Wynonna and the Big Noise drew thousands to a cow pasture near White Sulphur Springs for Red Ants Pants Festival.

Towns across the state close off streets for free weekly concerts that draw hundreds downtown — a surefire economic boon for the restaurants and retail stores nearby. And it's not uncommon in interstate-adjacent towns to find touring musicians without a gig busking for gas money.

Meanwhile, much of Montana's own contemporary music scene is linked to the state's past — less in terms of its musical influences than in terms of renovated venues that have been rescued from neglect or downright despair.

"There's a live-music renaissance going on in Montana," says Bozeman-based singer-songwriter Jason Wickens, who also produces the syndicated radio program *Live from the Divide.* "I'm also fascinated by the old, historic theaters in this state. And the microbreweries book a lot of high-profile musicians, too."

The elegant Alberta Bair Theater wears many hats in Billings, and Helena has the Motherlode. Bozeman boasts the Ellen Theatre and the less-grand Filling Station — an enduring dive bar known as

Band of Drifters

"The Filler" to locals. Glasgow has the marvelous Fort Peck Theatre nearby, while Anaconda has the Washoe, a gold-gilded, art deco, post-Depression architectural masterpiece. Most of these venues, and dozens of others, are enjoying a renaissance of sorts as Montana continues to grow in population.

Busy Bozeman

In many ways, Bozeman in southwest Montana is a microcosm of the state: It's eclectic and has long incubated its arts scene. The people who live there actively engage nature either through vocation or recreation, and the population is growing. In the 2015 census estimate, officials figured Bozeman to have about 43,400 people, not even enough to fill the average football stadium in the Southeastern Conference. Yet folks in this bucolic, high-desert town are worried about growth — Bozeman is the fastest-growing city in the state, and that's no wonder.

Bozeman is surrounded by the Rocky Mountains in every direction. Its Main

Street — notably void of national chain restaurants — has all the warmth and charm of Bedford Falls, sans Mr. Potter. While you're just as likely to find ranchers wearing dusty Wranglers at the Rocking R Bar as you are college students, this is no hick town. The co-op rivals Whole Foods in terms of pricey, organic farm-to-table fare, and the renovated Ellen Theatre is just as likely to draw large crowds for Western film retrospectives as it is for its surprisingly diverse musical performances — progressive folk artist Gregory Alan Isakov sold out the Ellen last summer.

The Whistle Pig, a tiny Korean restaurant downtown, pushes its tables aside every few weeks to make room for all-ages shows by local and touring punk bands alike. The Molly Brown, part pool hall, part casino catering to college students, offers hip-hop acts from time to time. And the Cat's Paw is a reliable stop-in for locals wanting to dance to a-little-too-loud cover tunes by pretty good local musicians who never quit their day jobs. Long ago the venue hosted

roots music favorites like Lucinda Williams and Anne McCue, and Dave Matthews played there before *Under the Table and Dreaming* catapulted him to much larger venues.

Meanwhile, Bozeman's Eagles Lodge draws in the dancers. Durable Naugahyde barstools surround a sizeable Formica-topped bar that forms an island around which college students can watch other college students mingle. More than a dozen hockey trophies are enshrined behind dusty glass above the bar. A piercing pedal steel guitar calls out from the back room. On any given night, Ian Thomas and his Band of Drifters have 25 couples up and two-stepping in a counterclockwise promenade, effortlessly slipping past the two inconveniently located metal support beams that bisect the dance floor. The older fellas are wearing pressed, snap-close plaid shirts tucked into their Wranglers, boots, and cowboy hats; bolo ties are optional. Despite being dressed come-as-you-are casual, the young bucks know the moves and can sashay with the

> "A lot of bands you might see in a big venue in Nashville or Austin — we have the opportunity to see them with 50 or so other people. Here, we're kind of sitting in their laps. And the artist is part of the same experience moreso than you might find in a larger community. We don't really have industry people who might sweep the artists into a bar with them after the set; we fans get to do that."
>
> Mike "Bueno" Good

best of them. The women, ranging from 21 to 70-something, are dressed to impress — some in jeans, some in knee-length dresses, some wearing loosely wrapped scarves around their necks, some without.

When an up-tempo song ends, the dance floor quickly empties. But the band has the unhurried confidence of a veteran of the dance-hall circuit. They know they're only getting started on a long night.

"The smaller towns, people are very appreciative to have music — when bands come through here, Montanans show up," says Thomas, 36, a lanky singer-songwriter who splits his time between Livingston and Knoxville, Tennessee. "When you're playing a bar in Montana, the gigs can run four hours. And it's a little more personal here, and there's less pretension. And when you get an out-of-stater here who brings with him pretension, it never works."

Nashville-based folksinger Todd Snider — about as unpretentious as they come — clearly knows how to make it work in Montana. His shows in Bozeman reliably sell out well in advance, perhaps in part because of his willingness to embrace the intimacy of his Montana audiences. Snider says he "got weird" a couple of years ago after a gig at the Filler.

"One night after we played at the Filling Station, we were trying to find this bonfire that was supposed to be the after party, and it turned out to be all the local bums, which actually turned out to be a great scene," Snider says. "It got late, and this one guy fell asleep and kind of rolled

into the fire, so we rolled him right back out and just kept the party going all night and into the next day. That afternoon, I got all the people at the bonfire laminates for the show. A while before it was time to go over to the show, we brought all those guys back to the hotel. Come to think of it, it seems like the hotel might have been kind of mad at us, and maybe that's why."

As Snider experienced on that unexpected night out, there's a certain *laissez faire* attitude among Montanans that lends itself to a special level of intimacy between artist and audience. Take Grammy-winner Bonnie Bishop's sold-out 2016 show at Live from the Divide, a tiny performance venue in Bozeman that distributes a syndicated radio show of the same name via NPR affiliates.

In a room that holds maybe 75 people, a late arrival awkwardly seated himself at a console no further than 18 inches from where she sat at a piano. Bishop joked about the proximity, but launched into the next song nonetheless. When the show was over, Bishop, her guitarist, and a few members of the audience made their way to a bar around the corner together for a few rounds of drinks.

According to Good of Cactus Records, that scene is typical of live music in Montana. "It's definitely intimate here in Montana," he says. "A lot of bands you might see in a big venue in Nashville or Austin — we have the opportunity to see them with 50 or so other people. Here, we're kind of sitting in their laps. And the artist is part of the same experience moreso than you might find in a larger

community. We don't really have industry people who might sweep the artists into a bar with them after the set; we fans get to do that."

'Music Church'

Bozeman is also home to Music Villa, a powerhouse retailer that *Guitar World* magazine recently ranked among the Top 10 guitar stores in the country. Locally owned, Music Villa prides itself on being a hub for a community of musicians rather than a place for musicians to part with their money. Professionals and hobbyists alike gather informally on Sundays to shoot the breeze, test-drive new merchandise, or check out the just-arrived used equipment. They call it "Music Church." James Taylor has been known to stop in when he's in town to play a house concert in nearby Big Sky. John Mayer and Jeff Bridges, each of whom have homes in the Livingston/Paradise Valley area, are also customers.

Bridges came to Paradise Valley in the early 1970s to film *Rancho Deluxe*. The Oscar-winning actor, who is also a notable musician — he fronts a band called the Abiders — met his future wife during the filming. A funky, creative scene was coalescing in the area around Livingston at the time, and Bridges decided to make his home there. The Livingston scene may have slowed down just a bit since the days when Hunter S. Thompson would descend upon the town for weeks at a time, and Jimmy Buffett moved away long ago. But the region just north of Yellowstone National Park remains a creative font for musicians and other creative types.

"There's a big upswell in music in Montana," Bridges says. "I met my dear friend [musician] Mike Divine up here nearly 40 years ago, and he's instrumental in the Livingston music scene. [Songwriter] Kostas is another dear friend from here, and we've played together a lot. 'Dobro Dick' Dillof, the Taylor Brothers, and Bill Payne [of Little Feat] all helped make this scene. The Abiders come up here and play. And, of course, we've got Gibson [acoustic guitars manufacturing plant in Bozeman]. And I also made *Rancho Deluxe, Thunderbolt and Lightfoot,* and a movie with Tom Waits called *Cold Feet,* written by Tom McGuane, here. John Mayer is part of the newer wave of musicians up here. Good music has been happening pretty consistently here in Montana ever since I got here — and before."

Jeremiah Slovack, an Emmy award-winning producer and sound engineer based in Bozeman, says he's not surprised some of the heavy-hitters who come here to perform decide to plant roots.

"These artists come here for a reason," Slovack says. "Their kids can go to a public school here because there's no paparazzi — it's respectful, it's quiet, it's non-invasive, and it's non-intrusive. Peter Fonda can ride his Indian up Main Street [in Big Sky], or Jeff Bridges will walk into the Music Villa like it's [his] store and pick up a guitar and play for a while. They're here so they can be just another person. These artists probably get bombarded in other cities, and they might be sick of that. It's just not that way here."

Inspirational Setting

In contrast to the growing wariness about overcrowding in booming Bozeman, Butte is offering tax incentives to ignite a much-needed cultural and economic renaissance. Nashville transplant Dave Goodwin purchased the historic Mountain View United Methodist Church on a hilltop downtown, near the famously giant pit of the town's copper mine. He is converting the gothic structure to a studio and performance venue.

"I bought the church because I wanted a space to record in," Goodwin says. "Most [churches] in Butte are abandoned and empty, but Mountain View was still functioning and wanted to sell. The size is right and the acoustics are amazing — I mean, like you rarely ever find."

Country music recording artist and actress Lari White came to Montana last summer to camp in Yellowstone with her husband, songwriter and producer Chuck Cannon, and their three teen/tween children. As many visitors from Nashville's music industry do when passing through southwest Montana, they stopped in to visit Goodwin, who took them to see Mountain View. Standing in the aisle, facing the massive pipes to the pump organ behind the altar, White found an auditory sweet spot. She interrupted the private tour to test the timbers with a Leonard Cohen classic.

"Haaaall-eee-luuu-iah!," she sang.

She turned to face the back of the room. Cannon, who has written hits for her as well as for Toby Keith, George Strait, and Wynonna, stood and joined in from a few pews back.

"Haaaall-eee-luuu-iah!"

Their children, each musically inclined, sang the verse.

I've heard there was a secret chord
That David played,
and it pleased the Lord...

"This room is great!" White exclaimed, to nobody in particular. Her progeny continued the song as White, Cannon, and Goodwin discussed the possibilities of a room like this.

Maybe it's the wooden pews. Maybe it's the stained glass. Maybe it's the plaster walls, or the sanctuary's soaring, two-story ceiling. But White is right; the room gave back everything the she and her family threw at it, swallowing none of the tone, delivering resonance and texture in return. After 143 years of hosting religious services, maybe the room has been kissed by God himself.

And perhaps Goodwin has captured what sets Montana's music scene apart: inspiration unfettered by the machine of the music business.

"The reason I wanted my studio to be in Montana is that I understood what nurturing is after I spent years writing songs inside four walls and a window across the street from other studios with four walls and a window," Goodwin says. "People come here and say, 'Man, this is how it should be.'" ∎

QUIET CORNERS AND EMPTY SPACES

Taking a page from Proust, the Jayhawks learn how to live for today

by Stacy Chandler

I'S HARD TO THINK OF A TOWN that's home to a more disparate list of musicians who made it big: the Replacements, Hüsker Dü, Soul Asylum, Babes in Toyland, and Prince all got their start in Minneapolis. Perhaps all the music is a product of the toughness that comes from the city's famously fierce winters, or an echo across the seemingly endless open spaces that unfurl not far from the bustling downtown. Maybe it's some magic coming off the lakes, or a vibe that resonates from "Minnesota nice" and all the term has come to imply.

In the 1980s, when the Jayhawks first came together, Minneapolis was fertile ground for a wide range of music — a dozen tiny scenes that worked together,

somehow, to form a larger, supportive whole. For a city to have a good music scene, says frontman Gary Louris, "they used to say you had to have a good record store, a great club, a great promoter, and a good radio station. And Minneapolis had all those." He cites the famed First Avenue and 7th St. Entry venues, along with the now-closed Oar Folkjokeopus record store, as particular tastemakers in the '80s music scene, adding, "it's always been kind of an arty town."

"All those things kind of mixed together with the fact that you're kind of isolated up there, you tend to be a little more reliant on your own scene to entertain yourself."

Marc Perlman, Jayhawks bassist and the only current member who's been in

the band since the very beginning (Louris joined a few weeks later), was raised in Minneapolis suburb St. Louis Park — home of songwriter/musician Dan Wilson, Sen. Al Franken, writer Thomas Friedman, and filmmakers the Coen Brothers. He says people in Minneapolis "have this aversion to being trendy and flashy and trying to be hip."

"If you were here back in the late '80s," he adds, "and you went and saw any of our bands, we were pretty much all wearing flannel shirts and jeans, because we just really weren't into fashion or flash or trying to be cool. And I think there's a real sense of honesty in the way we approach music and write. Minneapolis bands that I can remember never cared if their music fit into a

certain expectation. But it had to sound good to them; they never really cared what anybody else thought."

Given that, it's hard to imagine the Jayhawks out of the context of Minneapolis — and Louris and Perlman don't deny that the city had an impact on their sound.

"There seems to be something in our music that represents something very American," Louris says. "When we travel in Europe, people always say we seem to be a very definitive American band, and the music always is described as something that you can put on [during] a long road trip or driving at night in your car across some open areas.

"I think there's an openness, a less claustrophobic feel than maybe you get from some music from New York, or Europe, where people are more on top of each other. People are a little more spread out in the Midwest, and it tends to make the music more spread out."

"There's certainly some fucked-up things about people living in cold places," he adds, "and there's a lot of drinking at times in their lives, and that has certainly contributed to some sort of ramshackle vibe that happens in Midwestern music, where there's a looseness to it — almost a casualness — that tends to be a little more laid-back."

That casualness has been present in the Jayhawks' music from the very beginning, through all the band's lineups and evolutions. But listening to the group's latest album, 2016's *Paging Mr. Proust,* you can appreciate how far they've come.

"The first show we can remember playing together was at a kind of heavy metal/punk private kegger party at some house," recalls Perlman. "At the time, when the Jayhawks started, we were a little more punky than we are now, mostly because were weren't great musicians. And we just kind of played one speed — and it was fast."

But it wasn't long before the Jayhawks adjusted their course, realizing that together — with influences including rockabilly, folk, prog-rock, and punk — they made a sound all their own.

"There was something that was going on that was specific to Minneapolis," says Louris, "and I think we knew that our chemical makeup wasn't one that lent ourselves to be like the Replacements or Hüsker Dü. Certainly, I love those bands, but we found another way to express ourselves that felt like we weren't the baby band of those bands. [Mark] Olson and I both had kind of stumbled on this kind of roots music that seemed to be a new field for people like us, who were maybe not brought up out in the country."

Hold, Please

The Jayhawks' big break is the stuff of legend. Producer and American Recordings A&R guy George Drakoulias was on the phone with Dave Ayers at Minneapolis' Twin/Tone label when Ayers had to put down the phone for a minute. As Drakoulias waited on the other end of the line, he heard music playing in the background. Good music. Music so good that the conversation changed course when Ayers came back on the line.

"All I wanted to talk about was that sound," Drakoulias recounts in the liner notes for the 2011 reissue of the Jayhawks' 1992 breakthrough album,
Hollywood Town Hall. "Who were they? What were they? When could I see them?"

Drakoulias found answers for his questions and wound up producing that album for Def American Recordings, which later became American Recordings. He also produced its follow-up, *Tomorrow the Green Grass,* in early 1995. Meanwhile, the Jayhawks toured relentlessly, made some videos, and earned a place among alt-country royalty.

And then the bottom fell out.

In late 1995, the band was hard at work on the next album, with principal songwriters Louris and Olson trading songs and support as they had been all along. But a few sessions in, Olson walked away.

"When Mark walked out the door and tears were shed and words were spoken, I spent a couple days saying, 'This is a crossroads. Here's the chance I have to do something else,'" Louris told *No Depression* in 2000. " ... It's kinda like when you get a divorce and all of a sudden you think about those people you could have dated and now you can. But when the fantasies you may have entertained become reality, you realize they were better left as fantasy. And the reality was that I loved everybody in the band and wanted to continue."

So the Jayhawks forged ahead "destitute and shaken," as they sing in "Trouble," a song that spoke to the schism on 1997's *Sound of Lies,* the band's first post-Olson album. They developed a bold new sound that pulled in some electronic elements and marked a purposeful leap forward, though some early fans felt left behind.

> # "I think there's an openness, a less claustrophobic feel than maybe you get from some music from New York, or Europe, where people are more on top of each other. People are a little more spread out in the Midwest, and it tends to make the music more spread out."
>
> Gary Louris

"The band has always rejected that kind of mantle of being alt-country forefathers or the big gurus because I think they correctly saw that it's kind of an artistic limitation," says PD Larson, longtime friend of the band and also its archivist, sometime-manager, and "Swiss Army Knife," as he's listed in the liner notes of *Paging Mr. Proust*.

Subsequent albums and tours met with critical acclaim and gained a new generation of fans, and Olson's contributions, while lauded, were regarded as firmly in the past — until he came back.

Reunited, Olson and Louris launched an acoustic tour of Jayhawks music on their own in 2005, then toured in support of their duo album, *Ready for the Flood,* in 2009. In 2011, Olson was back in the full Jayhawks fold for *Mockingbird Time,* but the magic seemed to have flown. The album got a tepid reception, and the tour was visibly awkward until it finally derailed for good in 2012.

The Jayhawks went on a hiatus that no one — fans and band members alike — was sure would ever end. But like spring will surely come even after the coldest Minnesota winter, sooner or later, the Jayhawks emerged again.

The Proust Effect

Sometimes the smallest sensation — a passing whiff of a certain brand of soap or a snippet of song wafting out a window — will take you right back to an earlier time in your life, to a moment you'd nearly forgotten, or so you thought. For French author Marcel Proust, it was the taste of tea dipped with a bit of cake.

On a winter day, Proust came home feeling chilled and was offered a cup of tea by his mother, who also brought in a plate of petites madeleines. "Mechanically, weary after a dull day with the prospect of a depressing morrow," Proust dipped his cake in his tea and then took a sip — and he found himself transported. The taste brought to his mind the vivid memory of eating tea and cake with his aunt — a happy memory — and in turn he was flooded with memories of his childhood home and hometown. Such memories, unbidden from long ago and far away, are a theme in Proust's *In Search of Lost Time,* an exploration published in 1913 that coined the term "involuntary memory." That idea, which came to be called the Proust Effect, is still the subject of modern scientific study in the realms of memory and the human mind.

Proust, of course, had plenty more to say that is surprisingly relevant in modern life, and that, in part, is how his name ended up in the title of *Paging Mr. Proust.*

The title's seed was first planted when a friend of Louris' who was traveling in the Amsterdam airport told him she could swear she heard, above the din of people coming and going, Marcel Proust being paged by an airline.

"It just struck me," says Louris, who had been and still is reading Proust. "It wasn't just like sifting through the lyrics and finding a line, or coming up with something that sounds like an album title. It just seemed serendipitous. I just grabbed it, knowing that maybe I would get some shit for it for being so literary.

"But then it started working backward," he continues, the words tumbling fast. "It's kind of like how I write songs: I start writing and then I figure out what it's about. It explains some things about what I believe, that Proust says, that this album was kind of trying to preach a little bit, which is to slow down, be in the place you're at, be present, get away from what the world is about now, which is upgrades, updates, faster, smarter, faster, faster. 'Then we'll be happy,' that type of thing. People have lost the ability to be where they're at and be reflective. I think that explains some of the things that were bubbling under the song lyrics."

The airport setting stuck, too, both in the album packaging, which features a 1960s photo of the TWA terminal at New York's Idlewild Airport (now JFK), and in the movement-centered lyrics — including a trip through two airports on "Comeback Kids."

"There are a number of songs that do express some sort of movement, and that's just what life is, you know. You can't sit on your couch all day thinking about life," Louris says. "And my life is very dichotomous — I'm either moving every day, on tour, or I'm home, and then I kind of isolate in one spot. Life is like that, but some people just never stop. They just feel like it's a very American thing, too, to just stay busy, keep busy; it's almost like you need that to maintain distractions in your life so you don't have to stop and think. People don't process things now. I'm as guilty as anyone on that."

For years, part of Louris' process of processing involved pills — painkillers and Valium, specifically. After surgery in 2003, the pills became part of daily life, until he started rehab in 2012. Now, he says, he's learned to be still, at least figuratively, just as Proust was preaching.

"It took me a while to get back into writing," Louris says. "It's always good to give it a little time once you get off drugs, because the first songs you write are all like 'Ah, the world's great and everything's new,' and it kind of fades away a little bit. [Getting clean] just made me able to not bury myself in myself. I don't know if I had better ideas or not, but I certainly seemed to be more motivated and less cloudy. It gives you more clarity. There's a cliché about being fucked up and being creative. It can help sometimes, but in general, in the long run, I think it's just destructive. Being high doesn't equal being creative, necessarily. There are other ways to get past your conscious mind, which is basically what you're trying to do when you're trying to write in an inspired way."

Paging Mr. Proust, produced by Louris, Peter Buck, and Tucker Martine, is the result of sifting through a storehouse of Louris' songs, some of which he initially envisioned for a solo album but were, he came to realize, Jayhawks songs.

Much as in the aftermath of the 1995 split with Olson, after his 2012 departure, the band — and its fans — wondered if that was the end of the line. When the Jayhawks decided to keep going, "they really wanted to make the record they wanted to make," says Larson. "They didn't want to retrench to some imagined 'Jayhawks sound,' and they didn't want to just go off the deep end for the sake of going off the deep end."

What emerged was almost a compendium of the full range of Jayhawks sounds. Classic jangly guitar bubbles through lush harmonies on "Quiet Corners & Empty Spaces," fuzzed-up guitar pulses on "Lost the Summer," and a '60s throwback vibe sparkles on "Lovers of the Sun," and those are just the first three songs.

What's thoroughly modern about this record, though, is its funding. *Paging Mr. Proust* is marketed and distributed by Thirty Tigers, but it came into being through a crowdfunding campaign on PledgeMusic.

"I was a little bit reluctant to start asking for money," Louris admits, recalling fears that it would turn into a "garage sale." "But when it was explained to me that it was more like a preorder for people, it became more appealing. ... It worked out well: It made people feel involved, they got a bonus disc, and everybody was happy."

The band's share of that happiness carried through to their live shows supporting *Paging Mr. Proust* last year. In addition to Louris and Perlman, longtime Jayhawks Tim O'Reagan (on drums and singing) and Karen Grotberg (keyboards and harmonies) are back in the band, along with newcomer Chet Lyster, whom Louris credits with having "raised our game."

A lineup that clicks, some life lessons, and success at weathering the vagaries of an ever-changing music business have taken a lot of the pressure off, it seems, allowing the band to follow Proust's advice to take things slow and appreciate the now.

"We're a lot more relaxed now than we were in the past," Perlman says. "I think after 30 years, you don't worry as much about things as you did when you were starting out, especially when you were on major labels. It's just not as stressful as it used to be. We're enjoying playing for the sake of playing. Even though we still have to make a living off it, we're pretty comfortable where we are. It's not like we're worrying about having hits, worrying about the size of the venues we're playing, or worrying about whether people think we're cool or not. We just don't worry about that anymore. And that's very freeing." ∎

Gary Louris

Buck Owens and Roy Clark (L to R)

How "Hee Haw" brought down-home music and humor into the mainstream
by Lee Zimmerman

CORNPONE COUNTRY

> **"What I didn't know in the beginning was that it was a comedy show, with music added to it. It wasn't a country music show. It had these fast cuts, one after another, and music was simply the thread that kept it together. So if you didn't like one sketch, there would be something else coming along in another 30 seconds that maybe you would like. It was an ingenious way of presenting country music in a comedic arena."**
>
> Jim Halsey

Country wasn't king as far as the mainstream television audience was concerned when the '60s rolled into the '70s. With the Vietnam War taking its toll on America's mindset and the country still reeling in the aftermath of the Watergate scandal, the heartland and the homeland were far from in sync. Granted, rural programming had made inroads to some degree, as evidenced by the handful of relatively short-lived music variety shows such as *The Johnny Cash Show* and *The Glen Campbell Goodtime Hour*. But the networks' efforts proved most successful when it came to their slew of sitcoms — *The Andy Griffith Show, The Beverly Hillbillies,* and *Petticoat Junction* in particular. As Hollywood's attempt to create a kind of country culture crossover, those series proved ratings winners. But given the slapstick, the stereotypes, and the satire, it was hard for the average viewer to take any of it too seriously.

Enter *Hee Haw*.

Hosted by two credible country music stars, Buck Owens and Roy Clark, the show made its debut on CBS in the summer of 1969. Aside from its two frontmen, it featured an array of performers with substantial country cred, among them Roy Acuff, Tennessee Ernie Ford, Charlie McCoy, Barbi Benton, Grandpa Jones, George "Goober" Lindsey, Minnie Pearl, Junior Samples, Jeannie C. Riley, Buck Trent, and Owens' band the Buckaroos. The show was produced by TV and film guru Bernie Brillstein, whose other signature productions include *Saturday Night Live, The Larry Sanders Show, The Muppet Show,* and *The Sopranos.*

Originally developed as a summer replacement show for the recently canceled *The Smothers Brothers Comedy Hour* — a program that had always courted controversy and gotten under the skin of the CBS censors — *Hee Haw* at first appeared to be a continuation of the same but with one distinct difference: It lacked any political discourse. The network envisioned it as a way to continue the madcap variety format in which the Smothers Brothers had excelled, without the potentially troubling topics.

"It was a family-friendly show," recalls Buck Trent, an original member of the cast who appeared on the show for eight consecutive seasons. "They were trying to create a country version of *Laugh-In* that the whole family could sit down and watch without being embarrassed. Everyone understood the jokes. They all liked the music. There was a different guest host every week. We had all kinds of people come on the show — everyone from Kenny Rogers to Joe Frazier made appearances on the show. It was basic American entertainment, featuring the best country music of the day even before you could hear it on the radio."

Trent brought with him some solid credentials. A former member of Bill Monroe's Blue Grass Boys, he was the inventor of the electric banjo, a onetime regular performer on the *Grand Ole Opry*, and later a member of Porter Wagoner's backing band. He had also appeared on Roy Clark's daytime show prior to being enlisted for *Hee Haw*. In 1976, Trent toured the Soviet Union with Clark, becoming one of the first country musicians to play in that communist country.

Another of the key players who contributed to the show's creation was an artist manager named Jim Halsey. Halsey represented many of the biggest names in country music, several of whom — Clark, Minnie Pearl, and Grandpa Jones included — became integral members of the *Hee Haw* cast. Many of his other clients appeared on the show repeatedly as special guests.

"The producers of the show — Bernie Brillstein in particular — started talking to me about a year before we actually started shooting *Hee Haw*," Halsey remembers. "They told me they were working on a comedy show ... [and] he wanted Roy [Clark] to be a part of it. Roy had been doing mainstream television well before any other country artists. He had been on *The Tonight Show, Hollywood Palace, The Flip Wilson Show*. So when it came time to do *Hee Haw*, he already had a high recognition factor with TV audiences." Indeed, Clark was already a seasoned TV personality — he had previously hosted a daytime variety show on NBC and even played a pair of recurring roles on *The Beverly Hillbillies*.

Nevertheless, months went by before Halsey heard anything more. "I didn't think too much about it until the producers came back to me and said the Smothers Brothers show was going off the air for the summer and they wanted to do a one-hour, one-time special in the time slot.

"When we were halfway into shooting the special," he adds, "they came to me and told me the Smothers Brothers show had been canceled, and instead of one special, they needed nine [episodes of *Hee Haw*] as a summer replacement. Suddenly we had to work nine shows into our schedule on a weekly basis. But the timing was right, and in show business, that's what it's all about: the timing. People were ready for changes — politically, socially, and every other way."

The Formula Succeeds

Following its summer run, *Hee Haw* was given the go-ahead for a full season for fall. However, instead of embracing the show, many in the country music industry saw it as yet another substandard vehicle for perpetuating certain stereotypes — specifically, that of country bumpkins running around in overalls, touting their ties to the farm. "The people in Nashville said, 'Oh my God, they've set us back a hundred years,'" Buck Trent recalls. "They insisted

From left, Roy Clark, Lorne Greene, Minnie Pearl, and Grandpa Jones.

that we had to get away from all these hay bales! They wanted to go middle-of-the-road. Still, the show went over like wildfire, and then everyone wanted to be on it. It was hard to compete with a show that had everyone you had ever heard of [all together]."

Looking back, Halsey admits, "I didn't know if it was going to go over at all. One of the things Roy and I had been fighting against was the fact that whenever we did a show, whether it was *The Tonight Show* or *Bing Crosby* or *The Hollywood Palace*, they would always have a set that looked like a haystack or a barn. The producers would say, 'That image represents country music,' and I would say, 'No, it really doesn't.' They would ask me, 'How would you present Roy?' And I answered, 'Just like you would any other good artist.' So [then with *Hee Haw*,] here we had a show that's all about haystacks and barns."

While Halsey wasn't thrilled with the concept at first, he became more convinced that it would be the right vehicle for his talent once he delved into the producers' concept for the program.

"What I didn't know in the beginning was that it was a comedy show, with music added to it," he explains. "It wasn't a country music show. It had these fast cuts, one after another, and music was simply the thread that kept it together. So if you didn't like one sketch, there would be something else coming along in another 30 seconds that maybe you would like. It was an ingenious way of presenting country music in a comedic arena. ... We had no idea it was going to be the phenomenal success it was. It became one of the top three shows on the CBS network, along with *The Beverly Hillbillies* and *Green Acres.*"

Despite doing well in the ratings — *Hee Haw* ranked number 16 for the 1970-71 season — CBS dropped it in July 1971 as part of a purge that included other popular country comedies, among them *The Beverly Hillbillies, Green Acres,* and *Mayberry R.F.D.,* the successor to the ever-popular *The Andy Griffith Show.* With the new decade came a new direction. "CBS really didn't like that rural theme [anymore]," Halsey suggests. "They wanted to be known as an urban network."

New Life in Syndication

Though its network contract was cut short, *Hee Haw*'s producers continued to create episodes independently, which they then offered in syndication for the next 20 years, for any network to pick up. This followed the same method of independent syndication that *The Lawrence Welk Show* used after it was canceled by ABC. Ironically, the competition between the two inspired a hit novelty song called "The Lawrence Welk-Hee Haw Counter Revolution Polka" that brought Clark into the *Billboard* Country Music Top Ten in the fall of 1972. Clark and Owens continued to host *Hee Haw* jointly for another 15 years during its new phase of production until Owens decided to leave, turning the reins over to Clark and a revolving series of weekly guest hosts for the duration of its run.

Over the span of the new shows that were shot for syndication, *Hee Haw* evolved as a premiere showcase for a kind of country music that might otherwise have been overlooked by the masses. It offered a varied blend of authentic American roots music — from gospel and bluegrass to country and traditional rural tunes — all performed by some of the biggest stars of the day. Several guest artists appeared on each show, with Loretta Lynn and Garth Brooks among the many who made multiple appearances. Clogging groups, child singers, and the occasional pop performer also appeared from time to time, all in an effort to vary the template and reach a larger audience.

"We [felt] it was a hit everywhere we went," Halsey recalls. "When the show was on the air, we got that feedback from the audiences that we were playing to at the time, at the fairs and the music theaters. There's a kind of magic when certain moments come together, a magic that you can feel. Nobody has to tell you; you can just sense it."

Even so, *Hee Haw* eventually fell victim to a waning interest in the variety show format, and by the mid-1980s, the ratings began to plummet. By the early '90s, the death knell was near. An attempt to win over a younger demographic resulted in an altered format (which included dropping the barnyard sets in favor of more urban environs), along with a slight name change to *The Hee Haw Show.*

Unfortunately the strategy backfired; in their attempt to remake the program in a more youthful image, the producers only succeeded in alienating longtime fans. In a final attempt to salvage the show, it was revamped and retitled yet again, this time as *Hee Haw Silver,* both a bow to its 25th season and an excuse to rerun classic clips alongside a dwindling number of new skits. However, by the summer of 1992, the show had peaked and fizzled, and it left the airwaves altogether.

Nonetheless, *Hee Haw's* innovative approach lives on, through the artists who gained not only greater fame from the show but also the ability to play larger venues as a byproduct of that success. It represented a return to the rural values and all-American ideals that it shared week to week. Go to any Cracker Barrel restaurant and that theme still lingers. Visit Dollywood and the same ambience is there. On TV, episodes of the animated Fox series *Family Guy* occasionally feature cutaways of Conway Twitty singing in the *Hee Haw* style, sometimes using actual footage from the show.

Then there's Branson, Missouri, the place where several of the show's stars relocated in the early '80s, and where some still continue to perform to this day.

The Beginning of Branson

Branson has always prided itself on its down-home image. Early on, a music and comedy troupe called the

Baldknobbers, a group that took its name from the vigilantes who inhabited the Ozark Mountain region in the early 1900s, dressed in hillbilly costumes and performed on the street downtown. Eventually, those performances evolved into a popular theatrical revue and tourist attraction, starting an entertainment tradition that prospered for several decades. The Presley Family (no relation to Elvis or any of his kin) started their own jubilees, followed by the Mabes Family, who built a theater that became the Baldknobbers' permanent home. In its prime, the city was home to 50 theaters and dozens of shows that could be attended any night of the week.

Branson found itself with a direct *Hee Haw* connection, thanks to the Hee Haw Theater, which opened its doors in 1981. Even though it closed just two years later, the theater, with a troupe that included several former *Hee Haw* cast members performing shows that featured a similar mix of comedy and music, became a legitimate spin-off from the *Hee Haw* tradition.

Clark himself made a personal investment in Branson, licensing his name to the Roy Clark Celebrity Theatre and becoming the first bona fide country musician to have his own signature venue in the city. It not only provided him a steady secondary residency outside Las Vegas, where he had been performing with great success, but also it helped establish the city as a burgeoning magnet for live music. In fact, many of the first entertainers to play in Branson played at the Roy Clark Theatre, today known as the Hughes Brothers Theatre.

Other stars came to Branson as well, affirming the city's down-home brand. "Music [with a] patriotic theme, gospel, bluegrass, and comedy has always been the recipe for Branson's success," says Lynn Berry, director of communications for the Branson/Lakes Area Chamber of Commerce and Convention and Visitors Bureau. She's sure to point out that each of those musical traditions was also trumpeted by *Hee Haw*.

"Branson is all about wholesome family fun," says singer Susan Carmen, a former *Hee Haw* guest who still performs regularly in Branson. "Those are the things the city and the show have in common. They both embrace the same values and the same style of entertainment."

Not surprisingly then, in the early '80s, Branson began to evolve as a tourist mecca. The people who visited were by and large the same Midwest demographic that had been *Hee Haw*'s core audience. Soon, the city became known as an alternative to the pricey entertainment and casinos found in Las Vegas and Atlantic City — a far more affordable, accessible option.

One of those who came and stayed was Buck Trent. He first visited Branson in the early '80s while on tour with Porter Wagoner and soon thereafter secured an engagement as part of the resident cast of the Hee Haw Theater. When the theater closed, he became a regular performer at the Mickey Gilley Theatre, where he would often be the opening act for a visiting artist, performing three shows a day, seven days a week.

Then, in 1990, Trent became the first national act to host a morning radio program from Branson with his Buck Trent Country Music Show, which continues to be broadcast live five mornings a week from Branson's Jim Stafford Theater.

"We still play traditional country music, the kind of music people always used to like," Trent says. "Young people don't care what Mickey Gilley sings anymore. The radio isn't playing Ray Price or George Jones anymore. But in the show that we do, you'll hear that kind of music. There are people who still like traditional country music, because it's a kind of music that they understand."

Though his career has marched on, Trent still gets mileage from his time on *Hee Haw*. "It was a basic American-type show, and people still know it today," he says. "People still come up to me and say, 'I watch you every week on those *Hee Haw* reruns.'"

A Legacy that Lingers

In the early '90s, Branson saw a steady influx of big stars — major headliners Andy Williams, Charley Pride, Mel Tillis, Bobby Vinton, Johnny Mathis, and Ray Stevens — with the city's popularity further spurred on by a 1991 feature story on *60 Minutes*. Williams, Tillis, Stevens, Boxcar Willie, Mickey Gilley, and Moe Bandy, among others, established local connections with theaters that bore their names. These days, most of those stars have gone, leaving only a handful of venues that boast the names of major headliners.

Hee Haw, meanwhile, has also become something of anachronism, having fallen victim to evolving tastes and more sophisticated trends. "You couldn't do a *Hee Haw* show now," Trent laments. "It would be hard to imagine Tim McGraw jumping up out of the corner and telling a joke. ... *Hee Haw*'s humor simply wouldn't fly."

And yet, in its time, the show established a benchmark for country music like no other program had done before. "All of a sudden you had millions of people watching every Saturday night, and it made country music accessible to the world," Jim Halsey maintains. "It was a big breakthrough, not only for country music fans, but also for the people who never considered themselves country music fans. I remember Roy [Clark] and I went to meet with this big high-powered marketing company in New York, and when we got on the elevator, all these guys wearing suits and ties spied us and in unison they started yelling, 'Hee Haw!'

"It spoke to the common roots of everyone — country or urban, or whatever. Like *The Smothers Brothers Show* or *Laugh-In*, it had satire, but it was more about having a good time than making controversial statements or offering innuendos about politics. We were laughing at ourselves, and that was during a time when we all needed to do that — much like right now." ∎

This is the first installment in a four-part series by our No Depression Writing Fellow, Sarah Smarsh. She will spend 2017 writing about Dolly Parton. Read the next installments in the Summer, Fall, and Winter 2017 issues of this journal.

Illustration by Jenny Ritter

she come by it natural

Part One:

*How Dolly Parton grew to embody
the organic feminism of working-class women*

By Sarah Smarsh

When Dolly Parton's holiday movie about crises and miracles in East Tennessee — *Christmas of Many Colors: Circle of Love* — premiered on television last November, wildfires were burning up those Smoky Mountains where she first strummed a guitar. Most of the damage had been done over the previous two days, and as smoke cleared in Parton's native Sevier County, the death toll would reach 14. Tennessee Gov. Bill Haslam told *The New York Times* it was the biggest fire in the state in a century.

Hours before the film aired, Parton announced that her Dollywood Foundation would give a thousand dollars per month for six months to every family who lost their home. About 900 families would apply for the funds.

When I posted news of Parton's fire-victim fund to social media that evening, a West Virginia acquaintance and filmmaker who documents poverty in Appalachia commented, "My first words after the fires: Dolly will save 'em." As she typed this, 11.5 million people were tuning in to see Parton make a cameo appearance in *Christmas of Many Colors* — as a generous hooker shunned by self-proclaimed Christians in her hometown.

Much has been sung about auburn-haired "Jolene," the real-life siren Parton says worked at a bank and flirted with her husband when he came in to do business; she inspired the most covered of her hundreds of original recorded songs. But the woman to whom music owes much more is the blond "town tramp" Parton admired as a child. Parton created her look in that woman's image.

She had "yellow hair piled on top of her head, red lipstick, her eyes all painted up, and her clothes all tight and flashy," Parton recalled in a 2016 interview with *Southern Living*. "I just thought she was the prettiest thing I'd ever seen. And then when everybody said, 'Oh, she's just trash,' I thought, 'That's what I'm going to be when I grow up! Trash!'"

Parton, now 71, has told this story countless times because she is a woman whose appearance provokes people to demand an explanation. In *Christmas of Many Colors*, she finally pays full homage to the "painted lady" by making her the guardian angel of a narrative based loosely on a Christmas during Parton's childhood.

In the movie, young Dolly stands on a sidewalk strumming a guitar on a cold December night while holiday shoppers bustle along the main street of her tiny hometown; she's trying to help her dad and siblings come up with $69.95 — plus tax — to finally get her mom a gold wedding band. The yellow-haired woman, in her tight clothes and high heels, drops a 20-dollar bill into Dolly's guitar case, but a self-righteous shopkeeper sweeping the sidewalk refuses to let the elated child keep money tainted by the woman's sins.

"You get away from her," the outraged woman chides. "Why, this is a child of God. She don't want your dirty money." Before she sweeps her broom at the woman, she adds, "Comin' around decent folks all painted up, sticking out everywhere."

"Boy, you and that broom make a good team, you ol' witch," Parton's character replies before she clicks off into the darkness with an apology to young Dolly that she couldn't give her the money.

This signature Parton trifecta — eyebrow-raising tight clothes, generosity of heart, and a take-no-crap attitude — is an overlooked, unnamed sort of feminism I recognize in the hard-luck women who raised me. They didn't work as prostitutes, but they had the sort of lives that lead women down that path. Most of them left school in ninth, tenth, eleventh grade. There was no feminist literature or theory in our lives. There was only life, in which we were women — economically disenfranchised, working on our feet in restaurants and factories, and hopelessly sexualized.

My mom's long red acrylic fingernails, for example, didn't slow her down when she drove a UPS truck when I was a kid in the 1980s, dragging and pushing boxes of Christmas presents she and her own family wouldn't receive. Her other job was putting foundation on the faces of middle-class women at a makeup counter in a Wichita mall, a male manager stopping by to adjust the metal name tag pinned to her blouse. She knew exactly what was going on and neither liked it nor complained, the latter being risky business for a woman who must keep her job. She knew that the only way a woman with no money or connections can beat the game — that is to say, pay the bills for herself and her children — is by playing it.

In her songwriting, movie roles, and stage persona, Parton's exaltation of the strengths of this frequently vilified class of American woman is at once the greatest self-aware gender performance in modern history and a sincere expression of who Parton is. She stands for the poor woman, the working-class woman whose feminine sexuality is often an essential device for survival and yet whose tough presence might be considered "masculine" in corners of society where women haven't always worked, where the archaic concept of a "lady" lingers. They are single mothers in need of welfare and abortions, "uneducated" females with strong opinions, complicated people reduced to a meth-addict stereotype in the media. Long-shamed as a moral scourge in the US, they have precious few ambassadors to convey their grace.

What Parton has accomplished for feminism has less to do with feminism than it has to do with Parton, and she has everything to do with rural poverty. As my grandma would say about what alchemized a future legend in those Appalachian hills in the middle of the 20th century, she come by it natural.

Outta That Holler

The fourth of 12 siblings, Parton was born on a small farm in 1946; her father, Lee, paid the doctor a bag of grain for the delivery. As those familiar with her music know, growing up wearing dresses made of feed sacks didn't make her sorrowful but rather grateful — a fact that, paradoxically, has helped make her a very rich woman. The royalties for "Coat of Many Colors," her enduring 1971 song about cherishing a garment her mother sewed from rags in spite of being

> There was no feminist literature or theory in our lives. There was only life, in which we were women — economically disenfranchised, working on our feet in restaurants and factories, and hopelessly sexualized.

shamed for it at school, roll in year after year.

Of her many hits, Parton has described that tribute to her mother, Avie Lee, as the one most special to her. She says she got her musical talent from that side of her family, whom she describes as "dreamers." During Parton's childhood, radios, record players, and electricity hadn't yet reached the rural poor, and they entertained themselves in their own homes with old ways passed down from European country peasantry. Her maternal grandfather, a Pentecostal preacher, played fiddle and wrote songs.

Avie Lee's brother, Billy, played guitar — and noticed young Dolly's musical talent. He helped get her onto the legendary Knoxville radio and TV show *Cas Walker's Farm and Home Hour;* reportedly bought her first proper guitar, a child-sized acoustic Martin, when she was eight (replacing the one she'd made from an old mandolin and two found strings); and helped her write her first single, "Puppy Love," penned when she was 11 and recorded after a 30-hour bus ride to Goldband Records in Lake Charles, Louisiana, with her grandma in 1959, when she was 13.

By that time, rock and roll — rooted in Southern black culture — was sweeping white America and infusing even country sounds. It showed up in the uptempo dance beat of "Puppy Love" and in Uncle Billy's slick Elvis-style pompadour. Parton admired rockabilly pioneer Rose Maddox, the daughter of Alabama sharecroppers. But Appalachia's ancient melodies, the poor European cousin to slavery's African blues, were the songs that shaped her first. In one hit from her early career, "Apple Jack," which she has said portrays a composite of real people, she tells of visiting a mountain-music man who gifted her his banjo when he died — a bit of Africa that had reached East Tennessee over the centuries.

While Parton's musicianship and mentorship came from her mother's family, her business acumen, she says, came from her father — a tender-hearted lifelong laborer who didn't learn to read and write but nonetheless was savvy with a horse trade and could stretch a bit of money a long way. The sharp business mind that eventually built an empire worth hundreds of millions of dollars was also influenced by the premium her dad put on their humble home.

She described those seemingly conflicting interests — "getting out" and being where you most belong — onstage in Kansas City during her 2016 tour for her latest album, *Pure and Simple.* That production stripped away the razzle-dazzle of backup bands and big sets featured on so many of her tours, putting Parton instead on a mostly bare stage with three backup musicians and a few cascades of white fabric. The show started with the sound of crickets and bulbs blinking like lightning bugs.

At one point during the performance, Parton climbed a few steps to sit on a white platform described as a front porch but that turned out to be an elevated position for communing with heaven. Before singing "Smoky Mountain Memories," her 1978 song about poor workers drawn north during the midcentury factory boom, she paid tribute to her father's hard work, economic decisions, and commitment to his family.

"Lee, you oughta go up'air, get them kids outta that holler," she remembered people telling her dad. But after a short stint in Detroit when Parton was a child, Lee announced that he would die in the East Tennessee mountains. They wouldn't have much there, he knew, but they'd have food and shelter — and they'd be home.

Parton stood up with a flute to open the number. She couldn't sit while she performed it, she said, because her dad deserved a standing ovation. In an instant, thousands of people stood up — her audiences would do the Hokey Pokey if she asked — and Parton laughed.

"Not from you!" she said, and the crowd laughed with her. Then they sat down and cried while she sang.

Turning her attention to Avie Lee, Parton set up "Coat of Many Colors" with analogous tales of her mother's creativity in the face of deprivation. To boost the kids' spirits, Parton recalled, Avie would send them outside to pick the best rock for her to cook "stone soup" — always intending to select and praise the child who had the hardest day.

One imagines Parton, who told the crowd her family had running water "if we ran and got it," absorbed her wit and natural poetry from her mother's language. "If we had some ham, we'd have ham and eggs. If we had some eggs," Parton quoted her mom to the crowd.

These are stories Parton has told countless times over the decades — mind you, she spent 18 years in her parents' cabin, compared with 53 years in Nashville and beyond, most of which she has lived at the height of fame and fortune. But fans who have heard the anecdote a thousand times gladly line up to hear it a thousand and one, maybe because there are so few entertainers who truly own such experiences. You can recognize that ownership, by the way, by its humor.

Joking about poverty where more privileged people tend to mire it in precious sadness — a demonstration of their own sense of guilt or, perhaps, lacking understanding of what brings happiness — is a hallmark of women in poor spaces. Firsthand experience allows for a tale that's more complex than a somber lament. Those women never had to feign being impressed by things their husbands couldn't afford to give them, and in that gulf between one's reality and the middle-class images in magazine advertisements arises humor.

When my grandma recounted my biological grandfather's proposal to her when she became pregnant with my mother at age 16, for instance, it was with a laugh and a cigarette drag.

"It wasn't any of this, 'please be my darling wife.' Sheeeeit," she said, and we both cracked up — not at our own family's misfortunes but at the delusions of women who got a sentimental proposal and a big diamond before they spent a lifetime pushing a vacuum.

If you find Parton's work sentimental,

you haven't listened to much of it. Recurring motifs of her early songs, in particular, include hypocritical, violent, and even murderous men; women being used, neglected, and shamed; and dying children — the baby sibling Parton was charged with caring for as a child got sick and died. Known for her "fake" appearance — the wigs, the synthetic fabrics clinging to a surgically altered body, the acrylic nails in shades of yellow and pink — Parton can be a very dark realist when she writes. That darkness in a woman's voice, plain stories of hell on earth sung by women who have little to carry them forward but faith, is the divine feminine of American roots music.

"Little Sparrow," from her 2001 album by the same name, which blends the bluegrass, folk, and country gospel sounds of her native home, is sung in the voice of a jilted, devastated woman warning young girls to "never trust the hearts of men." As haunting as the melody is, Parton — who is given to undercutting serious moments with an endearing bit of nervous energy — sets it up with a joke onstage: "I call it my little sad-ass song."

Parton says you can't be from where she's from and not like woeful melodies. The worst stories she tells of those mountains in her songwriting seem to represent what she saw outside her family's house. The biggest grievance she has discussed about her domestic life is that her father wouldn't say "I love you" — a common cultural affliction for men of all classes in that period and, perhaps to a lesser degree, still today. But Parton insists that, in practice, her home was so rich in love that every material poverty was mitigated.

After the moving tribute to her musical mother and industrious father, at a stop on the same tour in Texas, Parton made her way down the steps of the "porch" before it was wheeled offstage.

"Time to come down from heaven, I reckon," she said, and a muscular, bare-armed man in a black vest and hat previously introduced as her "sexy cowboy" carried out a new instrument. (By this point, she had played guitar, dulcimer, and flute.) It was white and covered in rhinestones, like all her other instruments, including a grand piano she played for one number.

"Oh, the cowboy brought me a banjo," Parton said. Soon she was shredding

on it with her talon fingernails during "Rocky Top," a bluegrass song exalting the Tennessee hills written in 1967 by a married pair of innkeepers just up the road from Parton's hometown in Gatlinburg, the place hardest hit by the recent wildfires.

During the bridge, Parton slung the banjo over her back, and the cowboy handed her a fiddle. While the fast beat pulsed and one of her band members played another banjo, Parton tapped the air with her bow like a conductor. Right before her solo, she pointed the bow at the cowboy and said in time, like a jazz singer: "You dance." The sexy cowboy hooked his thumbs into the belt loops of his tight jeans and kicked up his heels in place while she fiddled and the crowd roared.

Parton spends more time than the average performer onstage deferring to others with what, by all known accounts, is a sincere humility — praising the crowd, thanking her own band, honoring her family and her roots. But at that moment in the show, tears still wet on faces after the poignant songs for mama and daddy, it was Parton's own delight, desires, and power on display. She sang the song, she played two instruments on the song, and the hot piece of man next to her was on her payroll — and when she said "dance," he danced.

Sex was the third formative pillar of her life alongside music and religion, Parton said in her 1994 autobiography, *My Life and Other Unfinished Business.* She used to haunt an abandoned chapel with broken windows and buckled floorboards where teenagers left condom wrappers under the porch; inside was a defunct piano and "dirty drawings" on the walls. In that space of music, sex, and God, Parton wrote, she experienced a spiritual epiphany that "it was all right for me to be a sexual being." Indeed, she has described herself as having been hormonally precocious both inside and out.

While famously lifted, nipped, and tucked over the years, her figure was just as improbable as it naturally developed. The resulting attention from males clued her in to her own sexual power at a young age, and she embraced it, dyeing her lips with iodine from the family medicine cabinet for lack of lipstick. This zeal for sexy behavior did not, in the eyes of her people's strict patriarchal religion, honor her father and her mother.

In a 2003 *Rolling Stone* interview, she

described her father punishing her for making herself up. " 'This is my natural color!' " she remembered insisting. "The more Daddy tried to rub it off, the redder it was. It's like, 'This red ass of yours after a whipping, is that your natural color?' Oh, I got lots of whippin's over makeup."

Her mom and preacher grandpa shuddered too, worried that only the devil would lead her to look like Jezebel. During her 1983 television special *Dolly in London,* Parton called herself "the original punk rocker." In the early '60s, as a teen, she pierced her own ears to hang feathers from them and ratted her hair. When her mother suggested she'd been possessed, Parton told her to give credit where it was due — not to Satan but to Dolly herself.

"I couldn't get my hair big enough or 'yaller' enough, couldn't get my skirt tight enough, my blouses low enough," she recalled in her autobiography. "... Of course, I had to get away from home to really put on the dog. I'd go into the four-for-a-quarter picture booth at Woolworth's, unbutton my blouse, push my headlights up with my arms and take pictures."

What women who didn't grow up on a farm might miss is that, where Parton was from, this common act of female adolescent rebellion wasn't just about attracting boys. It was about claiming her femininity in a place where everyone, male and female alike, summoned "masculine" attributes and downplayed "feminine" ones in order to survive.

"My sisters and I used to cling desperately to anything halfway feminine," Parton wrote. "We could see the pictures of the models in the newspapers that lined the walls of our house and the occasional glimpse we would get at a magazine. We wanted to look like them. They didn't look at all like they had to work in the fields. They didn't look like they had to take a spit bath in a dishpan."

For Parton, lipstick and store-bought clothing represented not just a life beyond menial labor but also a level of economic agency that might protect a woman from assault. Indeed, research indicates that the impoverished woman is more likely than her more affluent counterpart to experience severe violence at the hands of a man.

"Womanhood was a difficult thing to get a grip on in those hills, unless you were a man," Parton wrote. "[Glamorous women in magazines] didn't look as if men and boys could just put their hands on them any time they felt like it, and with any degree of roughness they chose. The way they looked, if a man wanted to touch them, he'd better be damned nice to them."

That's one viewpoint to which mistreated women of all classes can attest, to some extent, and which Parton surely enjoys now. Still, there's a hard truth to it. In the social climb to come, Parton had white skin, good health, and loads of talent on her side. But something the world values even less than a girl is a poor one.

My family's poverty was nothing like Parton's, but it was enough that I knew shame. We lived in rural Kansas, so I didn't feel it until I started school, where other children's clothes and lives were there for me to see and contrast with my own.

That reckoning began even before I reached the school on the first day: The bus pulled up to our long dirt driveway, and I climbed on with a paper grocery sack full of supplies. I had been in a state of bliss as my mother checked off the teacher-provided list she had in her purse with a small calculator and her plastic coupon organizer. But I was the only child on the bus whose supplies weren't in a backpack, and by the time we reached the school — nearly an hour-long drive after all the necessary stops, winding along dirt roads and ruts — I was embarrassed when I unloaded the new crayons and pencils I prized from a paper sack.

If you're a peaceful child, as I was, not given to throwing tantrums to process frustration, in such moments you have two choices: Hang your head and cry piteously so someone might feel sorry for you, or tilt your chin up and let the tears inside you turn into a salty form of power. The women I knew had taught me the latter skill — a particular strength for a female in that she will be called upon throughout her life to not only care for herself but also to care for others. Little room is left in such a life for one's own complaints.

The transmutation of pain into power is a feature of all musical genres and indeed all forms of art. For women in poverty, though, it is not just a song but a way of life, not just a performance but a necessity. As with Loretta Lynn, Tammy Wynette, Patsy Cline, and so many female country performers before and since, Parton's music expresses this.

Her special twist though, unlike most of the rest, is that she conveys it with palpable positivity and a smile — understanding so deeply the connection between a difficult past and a blessed present that her mission on stage and in life is to honor that tension in other people's lives.

She reminds her audiences that, no matter where they came from, everyone can identify with being shamed one way or another, and no one deserves it. Never be ashamed of your home, your family, yourself, your religion, she says, and adoring crowds applaud. One need look no further than her immense LGBTQ following to know that Parton's transformation from a slut-shamed, talented teenage bumpkin to entertainment superstar contains a universal struggle that has less to do with being Appalachian than with being human. If her presence and the appreciation it instills in people could be whittled to a phrase, it's "be what you are."

In order to deliver that message to the masses, though — in order to tell the stories of impoverished women where she was from — Parton would have to be the woman who left behind both poverty and place. That meant leaving the people she loved most, but it wasn't a tough decision.

In her autobiography she described going to see a traveling sideshow as a child and being stunned to recognize her cousin Myrtle made up to play the "alligator girl."

"I could understand her completely," Parton wrote. "After all, I wanted to leave the mountains too, and I wanted attention. She probably thought I was making fun or blowing her cover, but I just wanted to say, 'Hello, I understand. Be the alligator girl. Be whatever your dreams and your luck will let you be.'"

Parton's dreams involved becoming a star. She practiced on her guitar, put an empty tin can on a stick wedged between the boards of her family's front porch and performed for chickens. But, as far as stardom goes, it doesn't matter how well you play and sing if you're only doing it on your own front porch.

Luckily, Uncle Billy had a car. The driver's-side door was wired to keep it on the frame, so that he had to crawl in and out of the passenger side, but the car moved. Over the years, he'd drive Parton 200 miles east to Nashville to knock on doors. Record executives turned them

away, and they slept in his car — the next day always driving back to the farm, back to Sevier County.

Talking through Songs

A few years ago, Parton dedicated a room of photos and memorabilia at Dollywood, the theme park she opened in her home county in 1986, to Bill Owens. In a video recording viewed by many of the park's 2.5 million annual visitors, Parton sings a song to her Uncle Billy from a small screen.

In the song, she recalls the two of them dreaming of a world far beyond those hills after chores were done, and his abiding belief in her dreams and instruction toward them — how to pick, how to yodel, how to shake her fears, how to act in proper company. "You told me I was special," she sings, "and I took it to heart." With the chorus, she plainly states "I love you" over and over, the words her dad couldn't say and that Billy might have struggled with, too.

In part because of that Tennessee man's loving tutelage, though, Parton is now the most successful female artist in country music history. She has sold well over 100 million albums and is a member of the Songwriters Hall of Fame; since 1964, she has published more than 3,000 songs, from country to pop to bluegrass to gospel. She is one of six women to have received the Country Music Association award for entertainer of the year. On the heels of two successful TV movies, a series tracing her childhood is reportedly in development.

After more than 50 years in the business, Parton's 43rd solo album, *Pure and Simple,* debuted at number one on the *Billboard* country-album chart in August 2016 — her first time in that spot in a quarter century. Meanwhile, her music has gotten almost no radio play since the early '90s, when Nashville's pop-country sound made a dramatic shift away from twang. That didn't keep her fans from packing arenas during her biggest North American tour in 25 years, in more than 60 cities.

When I surprised my Grandma Betty with tickets to see that tour in Kansas City last summer, at age 71 — she and Parton were born eight months apart — she had never before been to a big arena concert. We are not, as noted, a family with money lying around for tickets to big shows. I had envisioned us wearing matching shirts and emptying a can of Aqua Net onto matching beehives for the occasion, but the trip and all it represented to us — for one thing, I guess, that we weren't as poor as we used to be — was overwhelming enough.

Aside from being the same age, Betty and Dolly share somewhat similar origins. They both had an outhouse at home — Betty's temporary, but an extreme class marker for her generation all the same. They both hated school and felt like outcasts there. Punk before punk was cool, Betty dyed her hair green on St. Patrick's Day when she was a 14-year-old waitress in Wichita; when the scandalized boss told her to go home, she refused to return rather than rinse the color out of her hair. As a young woman in the 1960s and '70s, Betty was a very hot number in big, blond wigs and miniskirts.

Betty fared a little better than Dolly with resources; her family had a car and a small house instead of a cabin, and there were four kids rather than 12. She drew a far worse hand than Dolly in the parents department, though. Her dad, a factory worker raised on a farm west of Wichita, was a violent alcoholic; her mom, a restaurant cook and sometime factory worker, was verbally abusive. It is perhaps for that reason that she went on to live firsthand the life that Parton apparently only observed and documented in song — the teenage pregnancy, the single motherhood, the violent husbands, the adult poverty.

When I was a kid, Betty would put one of Dolly's tapes in the deck of her old car while we rolled down some highway. It's the only music I remember her both singing and crying to in that emotionally repressed Midwestern culture and class, where both should only be done in private.

Watching the concert in Kansas City with Grandma Betty, whose farmhouse I moved into permanently when I was 11 years old and who was just 34 when she learned she'd be my grandmother, was like watching two women's lives with roughly similar beginnings but very different outcomes occupy the same space. I found myself watching Betty's reactions more than experiencing my own — a habit any creative spirit from a challenging home might share, as observation becomes a means of both distancing oneself in difficult moments and keeping an eye out for trouble. (People often ask me how, as a writer, I remember so much about my childhood,

and I suspect Parton's answer might be the same — if I was going to have a different sort of life, I had to take notes on the decisions and situations of those around me.)

Mostly during the concert, though, I was laughing.

"People ask me what it was like to work with Burt Reynolds," Parton said, only hinting that it would make a lot more sense to ask Reynolds what it was like to work with her. "Well, my best movie experiences were with women." At the mention of *Steel Magnolias* and *9 to 5*, the crowd thundered happily.

After the last note of her new song "Outside Your Door," in which a horny woman knocks on some door she apparently shouldn't be visiting, Parton said as an afterthought, "Open the dang door. You know you want it." The crowd laughed and cheered.

During a silence a man screamed, "I LOVE YOU DOLLYYYYYY." "I thought I told you to wait in the truck," she said — and even though she's used that line at every show since the Lyndon B. Johnson administration, the crowd laughed and cheered.

She fired her drummer for getting lippy, she explained, but that was OK because the keyboard had a drum machine on it, and it saved her thousands of dollars. The crowd laughed and cheered again.

"Jolene mighta worked at a bank," she said before starting in on that classic, "but I been to the bank many times with this here little song I wrote." The crowd laughed and visibly shook with particular fervor on that one.

Along the way, Betty laughed, too, but not the way she used to. Unlike Parton, she hasn't had good doctors keeping her well-oiled over the years, and her knees were aching in our cramped seats halfway up the enormous arena.

I got her to stand up and dance with me during "9 to 5," for which the whole place was on its feet near the end of the show, but a woman who lived the song

might not feel so jubilant.

In the 1970s, Betty got on as a secretary at the county courthouse in downtown Wichita, did a stint as one of the first female officers in the city's police reserves, and worked her way up to positions as a bailiff, subpoena officer, and probation officer for the criminal courts. She did it all as a blond woman men found attractive — and if you think that comes with a lot of perks, you've never been a woman in a courthouse full of men who are, in theory, the same ones who would represent you if you sued for sexual harassment.

I was so worried about whether Betty was enjoying herself, if only for knowing she was jonesing for a cigarette, that it took me a while to register that the concert was a pretty big deal for me, too. Though I grew up to be a live-music aficionado, following alt-country acts fervently and helping my then-husband, a professional guitar player, load in and out of bars for years, I had only been to one other mega-concert in my lifetime. The last instance was almost 30 years prior, in 1987, when my dad — a carpenter for whom such a show was also a once-in-a-lifetime deal — surprised me by taking me to see my favorite singer, Reba McEntire, play an arena on the eastern edge of Wichita.

We lived in the countryside to the west, amid the same wheat fields Dad grew up working, so the drive took us close to two hours. Once we got to the arena, McEntire was just a glittering, sequined speck from where we sat in the cheap nosebleeds. But it was such a momentous occasion for us that Dad took pictures of the stage with our 110-mm film camera to prove we'd been there while I sang along with every song.

After the concert, merchandise peddlers were out of kids' shirts, if they ever had any. So Dad stood in line to buy me all they had left — what was surely a wildly overpriced pink adult-size T-shirt with a broken heart on it and the name of one of McEntire's big singles at the time,

> That darkness in a woman's voice, plain stories of hell on earth sung by women who have little to carry them forward but faith, is the divine feminine of American roots music.

> What women who didn't grow up on a farm might miss is that, where Parton was from, this common act of female adolescent rebellion wasn't just about attracting boys. It was about claiming her femininity in a place where everyone, male and female alike, summoned "masculine" attributes and downplayed "feminine" ones in order to survive.

"What Am I Gonna Do About You." I used it as a blanket sleeping in his truck with my head on his lap on the long ride home through the dark country, and I wore it as a nightgown for the next two years.

The most poignant thing about that memory, for me, is that my dad — a very country boy, the youngest of six kids raised on a farm just down the road from the house he built us with his own hands, money for materials saved from a concrete-pouring business he ran for a few years — never liked country music.

"How do you listen to that stuff?" he used to say when my clock radio played 1980s pop-country first thing in the morning and I still needed to be prodded out of bed to catch the school bus. "It's so sad."

In my family, country music was foremost a language among women. It's how we talked to each other in a place where feelings weren't discussed.

"Listen to the words," Mom used to say, and the song on her record player, 8-track, or tape deck would convey some message about life, about men, about surviving. The voices belonged to Wynonna and Naomi Judd, K.T. Oslin, Janie Fricke, Lorrie Morgan, Anne Murray, and of course to Dolly, Tammy, Patsy, and Loretta. But the information passed from my mother to me, if only because she was connecting to those songs herself and I was there to hear them. I recall Reba's hit "Little Rock" — not about a town in Arkansas but about slipping a ring off one's finger — being on heavy rotation in our living room not long before my mom divorced my dad.

That I can map my upbringing against a soundtrack of declarative statements sung by women in denim and big hair is one of my greatest blessings,

I often think. We weren't a family of musicians, but the two women who raised me, my mom and grandma, cared a great deal about music that validated the stories of our lives — working-class girls, women, wives, mothers — in a way that TV shows, movies, books, magazines, and newspapers almost never did.

In the 1980s, when small prairie towns around us were dwindling with economic blight, living in the country meant frequent drives "to town" to buy this or that item or, say, to work at the Wichita mall over the holidays as my mom sometimes did for extra cash. That made for a lot of highway time, and instead of talking to each other, Mom and I both faced forward and sang the same words at the same time — country music, usually by women, filling the spaces of silence rolling along flat Kansas landscapes. Mom's cigarette smoke streamed out her cracked window while she held the steering wheel and tapped the air with one of her long, red fingernails.

One song we wore out on a tape together happens to be about women indirectly communicating with each other: "Letter Home," by the Forester Sisters, from their 1988 album "Sincerely." The lyrics are in the voice of a 29-year-old woman writing to tell her mom that her marriage is over.

One day when I was grown, it came on and we were delighted to find we both remembered all the words. Mom went quiet and listened at this verse in particular, though, like she was hearing it in a new way — now as the mother. And indeed at that moment I was the recently divorced, 30-ish daughter.

Jimmy found somebody else—

He told me that on New Year's Day.
He said he felt like a man with her,
And I watched them drive away.
Children and rent:
There was no time for tears,
Just time to carry on.
I didn't know how to tell you,
So there was no letter home.

Suddenly incredulous, Mom spoke. "He 'felt like a man with her, and I watched them drive away'?" she said. "How do you feel with this boot up your ass?"

We laughed so hard we doubled over. Neither of us needed to point out that every woman we knew, ourselves included, had only ever done the leaving, not the being left.

Mom stopped laughing again at the next verse, though.

I work in a place with
some other girls,
And we're all doin' alright.
We raise our kids,
and our jeans still fit,
And sometimes we go out at night.
I'm 29 years young today,
And I've lived it to the bone.
And I just wanted to send you
This letter home.

"Our jeans still fit," Mom said quietly and stared into the distance. "Yep." She slowly nodded her head, her smile gone and one eyebrow lifted in knowing.

What she knew was that the shape of a working-class woman's body has a lot to do with her survival. Not so much because she wants to "catch a man" — the men she has occasion to meet are broke, too, and don't think she doesn't know it — but because the significance of the female form as an object in society is one of the few powers she possesses. Unlike expensive college degrees and high-status material possessions, her body is hers, and how it looks will affect the economic course of her life: whether she looks nice enough to get the job at the makeup counter; whether the UPS manager, frowning that she's too small to do the work, can be convinced with a smile in the interview; whether the banker will approve the shaky loan.

(As it happens, the Forester Sisters' 1991 single "Men," which humorously paints a grim picture of the male gender, has been ironically used by Rush Limbaugh to set up his talk show's recurring "feminist update," which often derides women for their appearance.)

The physical stakes for the working-class woman go beyond those sexual undertones, even, to a matter of simple respect. Poor women are lampooned in popular culture as overweight, having bad teeth, bad clothes. All those signifiers of health and appearance — which of course are signifiers of class — affect every interaction in a woman's day. For the woman with no money in the bank, each of those interactions decides her and her family's survival.

One woman who understands that, of course, is Dolly Parton.

Parton's musical genius deserves a discussion far beyond and above the matters of gender and class. But the lyrics she wrote are forever tied to the body that sung them, her success forever tied to her having patterned her look after the "town trollop" of her native holler. For doing so, she received a fame laced with ridicule; during interviews in the 1970s and '80s, both Barbara Walters and Oprah Winfrey asked her to stand up so they could point out, incredulously and without humor, that she looked like a tramp.

Meanwhile, Johnny Cash famously wore black as a statement of rebellion against the status quo and on behalf of the downtrodden and was lauded for it. But that's the difference between being a man and a woman singing country-western music, or doing just about anything else.

The women who most deeply understand what Parton has been up to for half a century are the ones who don't have a voice, a platform, or a college education to articulate it. This too is a source of affection between Parton and some factions of her audience, perhaps — a secret that not one of hundreds, maybe thousands, of interviews has revealed, because people who make a living as writers and critics don't even know to ask the question: What role has Dolly Parton's music, movie roles, and persona played in the lives of economically disenfranchised women used to being shamed or cast as victims?

That question has a lot of correct answers, but one of them is this: At age 70, Dolly Parton produced a Christmas movie in which a shooed-away hooker returns at the end to help a little girl, and she cast herself to play the role.

It's widely discussed that Parton never forgot her roots, never left behind her community — the economy of which now revolves around her tourist attractions, the children of which receive books and scholarships her foundation provides, the recently incinerated homes of which will be rebuilt with her help. Less has been said about the extent to which she never left behind a certain archetype of American woman, the one whose trailer leads the world to deem her "trash." She isn't necessarily white, but she is necessarily poor, and she most definitely didn't get to study feminist theory in a college classroom.

Parton could've classed herself up decades ago, wearing less makeup as women who can afford it are given to doing, or singing about something that doesn't belong on the CD rack at Cracker Barrel. Instead she built her image and wrote her songs so that she can't sing a song or even look in the mirror without representing women who go unheard and unvalidated every day. The conversation between Parton and those women is in the music. They're somewhere wiping down mirrors in truck-stop diner restrooms, listening to country songs while they work.

The Great Unifier

One evening last June, before Betty and I saw Parton on tour, I was scrolling through Twitter, and Parton kept appearing in my feed. It was two days after the United Kingdom voted to withdraw from the European Union, sending cultural and economic shockwaves around the globe; one *New York Times* headline read, "Is 'Brexit' the Precursor to a Donald Trump Presidency?" (The column answered the question incorrectly, by the way.) A couple weeks prior, a gunman had killed 49 people in a gay nightclub in Orlando. In Washington, Democrats had just stormed the House floor to stage a sit-in for passage of gun-control legislation.

But, amid the dark political tweet-cloud on my computer screen, Parton appeared, holding a tiny bedazzled saxophone. A couple tweets down, here she was again, this time in a video singing 1960s protest songs a capella with her small band. Political tweet, political tweet — then Parton again! I realized that many of my friends in New York City were at her show in Queens.

She'd recently kicked off the Pure and Simple tour, which I hadn't even known was going on. I was confused — what were a bunch of New Yorkers doing knowing more about Dolly than I did?

The Dolly tweets piping in from New York City contacts were from a group that was diverse across lines of race, ethnicity, religion, and sexual orientation. They were all, however, women.

"That majestic bitch just started playing a goddamn PANFLUTE [sic]," one tweeted.

"Dolly Parton, sitting in a pew onstage, just got a stadium full of Nyers to shout 'Amen,'" said another. And then: "Nothing says #Pride like a stadium full of gays singing 'Here You Come Again' with Dolly Parton."

Suddenly two New York acquaintances I didn't realize knew one another were tweeting an exchange.

"Her voice is perfect."

"Dolly forever! Who knew she was such a storyteller?"

"About to fling myself at the stage."

At that moment, not yet having been among Parton's live audiences, I was amused, touched, and a little surprised. I've been chided about country music so many times that, when I lived for a couple years in New York, I hosted a party with the sole purpose of teaching people how to line dance and sending them home with a mix CD of something other than hipster-approved Johnny Cash. I guess I figured that Dolly Parton would only be loved ironically in some places.

I knew Parton was an icon beloved around the world, of course, but I hadn't realized the extent to which people who aren't "country" appreciate her, not just as a "crossover" artist but as the down-home, even religious persona she embodied in that recent tour. Perhaps the most remarkable thing about her steadfast focus on tales of poverty and rural life, sung from beneath a wig and rhinestones, is the extent to which she is universally adored for it, by people whose backgrounds couldn't be more different from hers.

My connection to Parton and her music, as a fellow working-class woman from the country, is but one facet of her boundless appeal, which is almost as inspiring to witness at her concerts as the performer herself. The diversity of people with even a passing affinity for her suggests that her true magic pertains not to scope — the global marketing efforts any wealthy star could attempt — but to her depth as an individual, and the space that creates for connection among seemingly unlikely friends.

Amid the crowds for last year's tour, Dolly drag queens turned and directed entire sections to sway with the beat. The people who swayed included wrinkled old people whose musical worlds revolve around the Grand Ole Opry, tortured urban teenagers wearing all black, little girls who discovered Parton through her goddaughter Miley Cyrus, groups of gay men who smell like cologne, college kids in American Apparel T-shirts that read "Dolly & Loretta & Patsy & Tammy," groups of men in T-shirts that read "proud redneck" with mud on their boots, lesbian couples holding hands, seen-it-all women like my Grandma Betty watching the stage quietly, and most everything in between.

Being among them, one sees and feels the power of a woman who truly lives the teachings of Jesus — love all, and judge not — in contrast to the hollow Christianity so much of Nashville's country music machine falsely espouses. It is an energy that cannot be faked; everyone there feels it, and Parton directly acknowledges it.

"Wouldn't it be nice if we could take a little vial of this love energy out there?" she asked an Austin crowd last December. People clapped and cried at the end of a very hard year in America, on the cusp of what was sure to be another hard one.

Parton almost always eschews politics, but she caught hell from both sides of the partisan divide last year for her approach to the presidential election. When *The New York Times* asked her what she thought about a woman running for president, Parton responded enthusiastically.

"Hillary might make as good a president as anybody ever has," she said. " ... I personally think a woman would do a great job. I think Hillary's very qualified. So if she gets it, I'll certainly be behind her."

Part of her conservative fan base shrieked in the blogosphere and social media, swearing they'd never buy her records or concert tickets again. Parton followed up with a statement to say that "if she gets it" referred to the presidency, not to the Democratic nomination, which wasn't yet official.

"My comment about supporting a woman in the White House was taken out of context," the statement read. She hadn't endorsed either candidate, she said, in future interviews taking the line that she hadn't even decided yet.

The left, then, shrieked at the idea that she would even consider a vote for Donald Trump, who by then was the Republican nominee. They, too, would never buy her records or concert tickets again.

The vast majority will probably keep on buying, of course. Parton is the great unifier not just across differences in identity and background but also across today's devastating political chasm. At her concerts over the last half of 2016, as the election climbed toward a fever pitch, perhaps the loudest applause was when she asked if she herself should run for president.

Parton then wove in her signature puns and self-deprecating jokes: Whether Clinton or Trump got in, the country would suffer from "PMS" either way — "presidential mood swings." She doesn't like to get political, but if she did run, she had the hair for it — it's huuuuuge. But then again maybe they didn't need any more boobs in the race.

Such crowd-pleasing diplomacy might have something to do with business, but Parton has put her sales on the line many times in the same political climate that saw the Dixie Chicks ostracized by Nashville and country radio when they denounced then-president George W. Bush after the 2003 invasion of Iraq.

In 2006, for example, after decades of vocal support for the LGBTQ community, she wrote a song for the *Transamerica* soundtrack, "Travelin' Thru." The song, which she performed at the Academy Awards when it was a best-song nominee, alludes to roots music about hard, transformative journeys, including the 19th century folk song "Wayfaring Stranger" and the early-20th century country gospel song "I Am a Pilgrim." Parton's soundtrack number weaves that history in as it honors the personal, public, and political struggles of people transitioning genders.

*We've all been crucified, and they
nailed Jesus to the tree,
And when I'm born again,
you're gonna see a change in me
God made me for a reason,
and nothing is in vain.
Redemption comes in many shapes
with many kinds of pain.*

Parton reportedly received death threats for participating in the movie. But she easily empathizes with those vilified or considered "freaks" for their experience of sexuality or gender, she has said, since even her experience as a cis-gender, straight woman contains parallels. She doesn't look like anyone else, for starters, and as a powerful woman she constantly is subjected to questions about her sex life. Rumors have swirled for years that she has a lesbian relationship with a childhood friend who is usually at her side. She insists she would proudly come out if that were the case; she has been married to the same man, a Tennessean who worked in the concrete business, for 50 years. What her LGBTQ fans respond to, she says, is not her own sexuality but her nonjudgmental embrace of theirs.

Parton's aversion to overt political discourse might have a lot to do with where she's from. Many members of my family don't like talking about politics either — not because they don't care, but because they aren't equipped with the particular language so often required to engage with the chattering class.

I am a professional communicator with three college degrees, and I have been shamed for using the wrong word or framework on Twitter — my view wasn't systemic enough, or my term wasn't the most frequent currency in intellectual jargon. Imagine if, like Parton and the women in my family, you hadn't been in school since you were a teenager in a rural area before the internet existed. I don't care how worldly you get; if that's your background, conversation dominated by people with college degrees is a space that will always feel intimidating or at least uncomfortable. See Parton's 2009 commencement speech at the University of Tennessee in which she admits that, for all the stages she has commanded, she is nervous speaking before an auditorium full of people in caps and gowns. Her voice shakes while she says it — a startling thing to watch in a woman whose profound confidence has publicly shone forth for decades.

Whatever Parton's reasons for conveying personal stories rather than polemics, that proclivity couldn't come at a better time in a world reeling with discord. Several of my friends — white, black, and Latina, with disparate class origins among them — commented in the weeks surrounding the presidential election that Parton was a balm of sorts, a spiritual leader when political leaders are failing.

Like any transcendent storyteller, her politics occur at the human level, examined as experience rather than

abstract concepts and lived directly rather than bandied about via pat academic terms. There is an important place for both the story that speaks for itself and the didactic argument. Parton exists in the former.

Last year she made a statement about race and immigration, not with words in a tweet but rather via the tone she set for her philanthropy to reach every victim of last year's Tennessee wildfires. According to Dollywood Foundation executive director Jeff Conyers, the organization was concerned that immigrants without legal status would forego applying for help; the foundation thus reached out to leaders in the Hispanic community to convey across language barriers that they weren't "out to catch" anyone. No questions were asked or records kept about race, ethnicity, or citizenship in connecting people with relief funds. In a similar vein, no reports or follow-ups are required from recipients; they are trusted to spend the assistance money however they wish.

I think again of my West Virginia friend's comment after the November 2016 Smoky Mountain wildfires: "Dolly will save 'em."

One reason she can do so, it seems, is that a lifetime of projecting love while staying off doctrine inspires good acts in others. Last December, she and her foundation put on an old-fashioned telethon — livestreamed online, as well — to raise money for the fire victims, and in a matter of hours they racked up $9 million. Performers who showed up when Parton called included country legends and (relative) country newcomers, including 1980s pop icon Cyndi Lauper and roots music superstar Chris Stapleton. Paul Simon called in with a $100,000 pledge while Parton was talking with Billy Ray Cyrus.

Parton has friends in many places. As I was typing this story in a Wichita coffee shop, a man who said he was homeless asked me what I was writing about. When I told him, he lit up and regaled me with Parton's life story, ending on a note of admiration for the integrity of her voice in an era of digitally manipulated music.

"She don't need none of that," he said. "No matter how many years pass and no matter what she looks like, her pipes are her pipes."

Maybe it's no coincidence that Parton's popularity seemed to surge the same year America seemed to falter. A fractured thing craves wholeness, and that's what Dolly Parton offers — one woman who simultaneously embodies

> Maybe it's no coincidence that Parton's popularity seemed to surge the same year America seemed to falter. A fractured thing craves wholeness, and that's what Dolly Parton offers — one woman who simultaneously embodies past and present, rich and poor, feminine and masculine, Jezebel and the Holy Mother, the journey of getting out and the sweet return to home.

past and present, rich and poor, feminine and masculine, Jezebel and the Holy Mother, the journey of getting out and the sweet return to home.

To quote one of my New York City acquaintances live-tweeting from Parton's show last June, "This is just everything."

The Last Laugh

Parton jokes that she had to get rich to sing like she was poor again. She also had to get out of a place where women could only be mothers and laborers in order to be a mother of sorts to the world. She might be an iconic artist and sexpot, but all along she has quietly shared and leveraged her wealth for the benefit of others. Most people have never heard of her Imagination Library, for instance, which each month gives a book to more than a million children around the world and reports that it has put over 80 million free books into the hands of children since 1995. She wears tight clothes in that context, too — the painted lady who comes bearing gifts. But the kids in that program don't make boob jokes. They call her "the book lady." A phrase a friend recently used to describe the host of a public radio show about spirituality seems to apply, when inner truth so surpasses our stereotypes about its container: "one of the few living astral moms."

Down in that holler in the middle of the 20th century, she was the same spirit inside a gifted poor girl. She had a loving family, a guitar, and an uncle for a mentor, and she longed to get gone to wherever she would be seen. She couldn't leave before she turned 18, she has said, because she figured her daddy would send a posse after her. So she suffered through high

school having the kind of body that can ruin a girl's life if she gets to believing that her body is all she's worth. Parton knew she was worth far more.

When she graduated from Sevier County High in 1964 — the first person from her family to earn a diploma — each member of the class was asked to stand up and share their plans. As she would recount in her University of Tennessee commencement address, she told her classmates she was going to Nashville to become a star. They burst out in laughter.

The next day, she hugged her family goodbye and went to the bus station.

In years to come, what she experienced in East Tennessee would be a foundation for her songwriting, a guidebook for carefully handling Nashville's men in suits, and a summons to share wealth with people who needed it — children, in particular. While waiting for that bus, her life was on the cusp of great change, and so was the world. Within weeks, the Civil Rights Act would be signed into law. The biggest women's movement since the fight for suffrage was brewing.

Parton didn't know all that. All she knew was that she was moving to a big, new place to do something she'd already been working toward for years. She carried everything she owned in her hands; somewhere deeper, she carried a belief that she was worth more than the world had suggested and an abiding humor about what she had suffered along the way.

"I boarded a Greyhound bus with my dreams, my old guitar, the songs I had written," she said in her autobiography, setting up a joke she has told many times, "and the rest of my belongings in a set of matching luggage — three paper bags from the same grocery store." ∎

NO DEPRESSION

If you've enjoyed reading this issue of *No Depression*, **subscribe now** and get the next four issues for just $47 (35% off retail).

Parekh & Singh

nodepression.com/subscribe

SUMMER: "The International Issue"
Available May 2017

Talk of international music often veers either toward vague "world music" or the ways in which artists around the world interpret American music. Here at No Depression, though, we prefer to focus on how traditional music is being updated to inspire new art. So, for our international issue, we're exploring music culture around the world, seeking innovative artists who revitalize tradition for contemporary audiences. Among them: Aboriginal songwriters in Australia who blend indigenous music culture with acoustic guitars, a Chinese band that attacks ancient-style stringed instruments with punk-like fervor, an American expat who has found a new voice over a decade in Argentina, and so on.

In this issue:
Street music culture in Cuba / Umbria, Italy's annual jazz festival / In Argentina with Richard Shindell and friends / Parekh & Singh and India's singer-songwriter scene / David Broza on the music of Israel and Palestine / Abigail Washburn interviews Hanggai / The progenitors of Original Pilipino Music (OPM) / Aboriginal singer-songwriters in Australia, and much more

Other issues in 2017:
Fall 2017: Roots & Branches spotlight on Emmylou Harris
Winter 2017: Singer-Songwriters

Richard Shindell

Hanggai

Contributors

ALLISON MOORER is a music industry veteran who has been nominated for Academy, Grammy, Americana Music Association, and Academy of Country Music awards. Her writing has appeared in *Guernica, Performing Songwriter,* and elsewhere. She is an MFA candidate in nonfiction at the New School in New York City, where she lives with her son.

ANNE MARGARET DANIEL teaches literature at the New School in New York City. Her writing about Oscar Wilde's trials, Bob Dylan, and contemporary music have been widely published. She is currently finishing a book about F. Scott Fitzgerald. She lives in Manhattan and upstate New York with her husband.

COLIN SUTHERLAND is an illustrator and designer living in the mountains of North Carolina. He finds inspiration in century-old fiddle tunes, vintage print ephemera, and the bawl of his bluetick coonhound.

CORBIE HILL is a freelance journalist who lives and works on three wooded acres in Pittsboro, North Carolina, with his wife and two daughters. He is afraid of heights.

DON MCLEESE has been a critic for the *Chicago Sun-Times* and *the Austin American-Statesman*, a frequent contributor to *Rolling Stone,* and a senior editor for the former incarnation of *No Depression*. His most recent book is *Dwight Yoakam: A Thousand Miles From Nowhere*. Don is a journalism professor at the University of Iowa.

DREW CHRISTIE is a Seattle-based animator and illustrator. His work has been featured by *The New York Times, Huffington Post, The Atlantic*, and others.

ERIN LYNDAL MARTIN received her MFA in poetry from the University of Alabama. Her work has appeared in *The Rumpus, Salon, The Quietus,* and elsewhere. Her favorite things are birthday cake and napping with the air conditioner on.

GRETA SONGE is an illustrator based in Coralville, Iowa. She earned an MFA in painting and drawing from the University of Iowa in 2004 and is an assistant professor of art at Kirkwood Community College in Cedar Rapids.

GWENDOLYN ELLIOTT is a freelance writer and former music editor of *Seattle Weekly*. She lives in the Emerald City with her husband, pets, and a lot of vinyl records.

HILARY SAUNDERS is the assistant music editor at *Paste* magazine, as well as a full-time freelance writer. She's written about arts and culture for publications around the world and is an un-ironic believer that rock and roll can save the world.

JENNY RITTER is one of those full-time musicians who still needs a creative hobby, so you'll find her acrylic and ink illustrations popping up all over the music world. This wearer of many hats leads a band under her own name and runs a couple of rock and roll choirs in Vancouver, British Columbia.

JONATHAN BERNSTEIN is a writer and fact-checker living in Brooklyn. His work has been published in *Oxford American, The Guardian, Rolling Stone, Pitchfork,* and *American Songwriter.*

JUSTIN MARABLE resides in Lawrence, Kansas, with his wife and three daughters. His work is included in various private and public collections nationwide and has appeared in local, regional, and national publications.

KATHERINE TURMAN is co-author of the book *Louder Than Hell: The Definitive Oral History of Metal* (HarperCollins) and has produced the syndicated classic rock radio show "Nights with Alice Cooper" since 2006. Her writing has appeared in the *Los Angeles Times, Rolling Stone, Billboard, Mother Jones, Esquire.com, Spin,* and *Village Voice.*

KEVIN LYNCH has won Milwaukee Press Club awards for best arts criticism and was principal writer of a *Milwaukee Journal* Newspapers in Education series on jazz that was nominated for a Pulitzer. He's written for *Down Beat, The Village Voice, The Chicago Tribune, and New Art Examiner,* and authored the forthcoming book *Voices in the River: The Jazz Message to Democracy.*

KIM RUEHL spent her 20s chasing the songwriter dream before falling into a career as a writer and editor. She is the editor-in-chief of *No Depression*, and her work has appeared in *Seattle Weekly, Billboard, NPR,* and elsewhere. She lives in Asheville, North Carolina, with her wife and daughter.

LEE ZIMMERMAN has been a freelance writer for publications like *American Songwriter, Blurt,* and *Billboard* for 20 years. He lives in Maryville, Tennessee, with his wife.

ROBBIE FULKS is a Grammy-nominated singer-songwriter based in Chicago. He attended Columbia College in New York City in 1980 and dropped out in 1982 to focus on the Greenwich Village songwriter scene and other ill-advised pursuits. He has released a dozen albums since his 1996 solo debut.

REVEREND PEYTON is the lead singer of a three-piece country-blues band from Brown County, Indiana, called the Reverend Peyton's Big Damn Band. Their most recent release was 2015's *So Delicious* on Yazoo Records.

SARAH SMARSH is a journalist who writes about socioeconomic class in America. She has reported on public policy for *Harper's,* NewYorker.com, *The Guardian, Guernica,* and others. Her essays on cultural boundaries have been published by *Aeon, McSweeney's,* and more. She formerly reviewed female country acts for alt-weeklies in the Midwest. Smarsh's book on the working poor and her upbringing in rural Kansas is forthcoming from Scribner. She lives in Kansas and Texas.

STACY CHANDLER is the assistant editor of *No Depression*. She is a freelance journalist living in Raleigh, North Carolina, with her husband, their daughter, a big dumb yellow dog, and a fiddle. She would like to thank Robbie Fulks for introducing her to the word "persiflage."

STEPHEN DEUSNER is a Tennessee native now living in Bloomington, Indiana. His work appears regularly in *Pitchfork, American Songwriter, Uncut, the Bluegrass Situation,* Stereogum, Salon, and elsewhere.

Screen Door

MIDWESTERN FOR LIFE

BY CHARLIE PARR

A few years back in Duluth, Minnesota, where I live, there was a snowstorm that put about three feet of snow on the ground in about 36 hours. I was home, and scheduled to play my usual hometown residency with a couple of friends. Nobody thought too much about it. The plows were off the streets because the snow was coming too fast, and the kids were snowboarding down Lake Avenue. There was no point in shoveling 'til the snow let up, so it was natural to get yourself out to the bar and see how everybody else was doing, and I thought we ought to be playing some music for 'em. So we piled into a neighbor's 4x4 and followed snowmobile tracks to the bar, where we found skis and snowshoes and sleds and ATVs outside and parkas on the floor in the hall and we played our hardest right up 'til they closed.

The best shows I've ever played are like that one, when I feel like I'm a part of this community, this kind of overgrown neighborhood, no matter where that happens. Usually it happens best in out-of-the-way places like Duluth, or Menomonie, Wisconsin, or Fargo, North Dakota, or Ames, Iowa, or Hancock, Michigan, and it feels like folks have made an effort to be there just like I have and the edge of the stage disappears a little and you find yourself having bits of conversation between the songs. "Where'd you come in from?" "Didja hit much snow on the way?" "Thanks for making it out this way."

The thought of moving out of Minnesota has never really occurred to me. I've been lucky enough to have traveled a lot, around the US and abroad, for the last 14 years without actually having a job, and I've never seriously said to myself, "I could do this from someplace else, someplace warmer, someplace closer to somewhere else."

I've known plenty of folks who feel like they need to be closer to where the action is, and plenty more who've gone there and returned home with the same music they had when they left, along with a bunch of good stories and maybe a little extra sadness. I can only speak for myself, and I know that I'm not exceptional in any way, but music is all I've ever been after and I found it at home from an early age. I know that's very lucky, and I'm grateful for that, and I also know that as I travel around the Midwest I'm constantly blown away by the music I hear not even five hours from my home. It seems like it's everywhere. It comes from little towns in the Driftless to no town at all in the Big Empty to historic neighborhoods like the West Bank in Minneapolis, from carpenters or miners who like to pick a little on the weekends to bona fide legends like "Spider" John Koerner or Prince or Paul Westerberg or Cornbread Harris.

I could leave here. Anytime I want. I love California and I could go there and be warm and sit by the sea. Or I could go to New York City. I love it there too, and I might be able to find my way or maybe not, I've heard it's tough out there. But I don't want to. I don't want to leave here. I've been spoiled by sad songs sung by drunken loggers on open mic night, by late night dancers at summer festivals along the Mississippi River, by rowdy gigs in tiny towns in the middle of nowhere, or gigs in the city that no one showed up to but you played better than ever, by our closeness and our community of oddball musicians and artists who at any given moment are students and truck drivers and cashiers and hairdressers and locomotive engineers and mentors and confidantes, dressed one minute in mukluks and the next in sneakers. I love it here. It's my home. It's as good as anywhere else.